John H. Westerhoff III

Building God's People

in a Materialistic Society

The Seabury Press / New York

1983
The Seabury Press
815 Second Avenue
New York, N.Y. 10017

Copyright © 1983 by John H. Westerhoff III

Printed in the United States of America

Library of Congress Cataloging in Publication Data
Westerhoff, John H.
  Building God's people in a materialistic society.
  (Schaff lectures at Pittsburgh Theological Seminary; 1980)
  Bibliography: p. 147
  1. Christian education—Addresses, essays, lectures.
2. Chrisitan life—1960- —Addresses, essays,
lectures. 3. Stewardship, Christian—Addresses, essays,
lectures. I. Title. II. Series.
BV1473.W46 1983   286   82-19592
ISBN 0-8164-2466-7

Acknowledgments

The material in this book
was first delivered as
the Schaff Lectures at Pittsburgh Theological Seminary
March 15–17, 1980.
Appreciation is acknowledged
for this honor and opportunity.

Dedicated to
Barnie,
my wife and faithful companion of twenty-five years;
and Jill, Jack, and Beth,
our children, the blessings of our love;
to the bishops, priests, deacons, and people
of the Episcopal Church,
our closest kin in Christ—
especially William Jones, my ordaining bishop;
the late Dean Urban T. Holmes, my mentor;
Robert Estill, my bishop; and Peter Lee, my rector—
and
to all those in the Christian family
who care about children enough
to be concerned about the lives of maturing adults.

Contents

Preface

The scope and subject of this book are something of a departure from my previous work, and a word of explanation seems in order.

Two years ago I was invited to give the Schaff Lectures at the Pittsburgh Theological Seminary of the United Presbyterian Church in the United States of America. I was struggling at the time with how Christian education fit into the present theological encyclopedia of the seminary. Since I first joined a theological faculty nine years ago, I had been troubled by the professional understanding of ministry that emerged in the church a quarter of a century ago and its resulting seminary curriculum. Caught between an understanding of profession as a response to a personal call from God along with a corresponding recognition of personal charisma (a God-given grace) by the church, and a modern secular view of profession as the possession of specialized knowledge and skills, the clergy appeared to have moved uncritically into the mainstream of modern history. Indeed, today most clergy understand themselves as professionals and the Doctor of Ministry degree has formalized the credentialing process for the "profession": ministry. Further, a specialized lay ministry, the professional Christian educator, emerged and resulted in a growing lack of interest among clergy in the church's educational ministry. As one ordained to the ministe-

rial priesthood in the Episcopal Church and engaged in the formation of future clergy in a United Methodist divinity school I have
experienced the dis-ease of these developments. I wanted to use the
opportunity of the Schaff Lectures to explore an alternative.

Then a year ago the Reverend Thomas Carson, executive for
stewardship in the Episcopal Church, invited me to write a book
that would provide assistance to parish Christian education programs in the teaching of sound principles of stewardship, especially
to aid children in the practice of stewardship during their maturing
years. Avery Brooke, my publisher at Seabury Press, and Donald
Kraus, my onetime student at Harvard Divinity School and now
my editor, encouraged me to accept.

When I began, the working title for this book was "Materialism
and Children." As such, it would have followed naturally in the
line of *Values for Tomorrow's Children, Will Our Children Have
Faith?* and *Bringing up Children in the Christian Faith*. However, as I
began to write, I discovered that I was writing more about a mature
community of adults sharing a life of stewardship with children
than about materialism and children. A short investigation of books
on stewardship in the Duke Divinity School library brought me up
short. Why were there so few books on such an important aspect of
ministry, why did most of them connect stewardship solely with
fund raising and church finance, and why could I not find one significant work on stewardship and Christian education? I thought, I
don't know enough to write such a book. My mind swirled with
questions and against my own best judgment I decided to give it a
try. However, the more I reflected on stewardship education, the
more I found myself driven back to the place of education in the
theological encyclopedia. That, I hope, explains the nature of this
little book. It was written, like all my others, in the spirit of an old
Hasidic tale about the well-known Rabbi Zaddok, who has been
lost in the wilderness most of his life. One day, a group of pilgrims

passing through this same wilderness also get lost. They are frightened until they spy Rabbi Zaddok. With hope in their eyes they run off to greet him. "Rabbi Zaddock, can you help us find the way out?" they cry. And he responds, "That I cannot do, but I do know one hundred trails that lead farther into the wilderness and perhaps if I share those with you, together we can find the way out."

Chapter One

Human Life in Dialogue with the Christian Story: Practical Theology

In our culture most people would rather act than reflect. Anti-intellectual attitudes toward religion are a characteristic trait. Pietism—an excessive concern for individual religious experience—and moralism—an excessive concern for individual right behavior—continue to plague the contemporary church in the United States. Hard theological thinking is not a popular activity in the typical parish church. Still, lest we fall into some historic heresy or be less than faithful to our potential as thinking persons, we need to acknowledge the crucial importance of rational reflection and learn to think theologically.

Flannery O'Connor, the novelist, wrote in one of her letters to a friend, "If you want your faith you have to work for it. It is a gift, but for very few is it a gift without any demand for equal time devoted to its cultivation. . . . To find out about faith you have to go to people who have it and you had better go to the most intellectual ones. . . .

I believe what the church teaches—that God has given us reason to use and that it will lead us toward a knowledge of him. . . ."[1]

Dame Julian, one of the great fourteenth-century English mystics, reflecting upon a series of divine "showings," as she called them, wrote: "Man endures in this life by three things, by which three God is honored and we are furthered, protected and saved. *The first is the use of man's natural reason*. The second is the common teaching of Holy Church. The third is the inward grace-giving operation of the Holy Spirit; and these three are all from one God" (italics mine).[2]

Education to be Christian assumes an awareness of the process by which we make rational sense of ourselves and our world. This process is an exploration of experience, an exploration guided by reason and illumined by our corporate memory; it is ultimately theological because it inevitably points to an infinite, yet-to-be-known God. Theological reflection is the explicit affirmation and exploration of the God-ward implications of all human effort to understand and live our lives—it is a mature, rational process.

We urgently need to help adults become more adult. The educational ministry of the church must be directed toward the living of a mature adult human life. Christian maturity demands the development of every aspect of our lives as thinking, feeling, and willing persons. Faith is a gift of God; theology is a human work, a deliberate, rational, reflective activity. Theology literally means talking rationally about God; its goal is knowledge and understanding through a critical inquiry into the meaning of faith. As such it demands a patient, laborious, and at times tedious engagement of the mind. To the limit of our intellectual potential every mature adult Christian is obliged to think theologically.

The processes of thinking theologically used to be divided into three levels of reflection and discourse known as fundamental, constructive, and practical theology. While this book intends to focus solely on practical theology and indeed on only one dimension of it, the catechetical, we need to identify and describe briefly the other two.

Fundamental Theology: Sometimes known as dogmatic theology, fundamental theology operates on that foundational level of reflection and discourse which provides us with an intellectual description, explication, and justification for the Christian faith. As such, it provides an introduction to the idea of Christianity and to the meaning of being Christian. A fundamental theology, such as Karl Rahner's *Foundations of Christian Faith* (published by Crossroad), explores the Christian tradition as it is found in the teachings of the early church fathers, especially as expressed in the Apostles' and Nicene Creeds and in the Word of God as conveyed in the Holy Scriptures. Through an exposition of this tradition, fundamental theology is written.

Christians are not free to believe anything they like and Christian ministers are not free to preach their private opinions. To be a mature Christian is to know and affirm the tradition once delivered to the saints. One Christian is no Christian. Personal convictions do not make one a Christian. Christian existence presumes and implies an incorporation into a community and its tradition. Christianity means a common life and a common belief. As Saint Vincent of Lérins said in a famous dictum, characteristic of the ancient church, "We must hold what has been believed everywhere, always, and by all."

Central to this tradition is the Apostles' Creed, that "rule of faith" into which we are initiated at our baptismal profession. And as Saint Irenaeus wrote, it is this rule of faith that must guide our reading and interpretation of the Scripture. The Bible is an essential aspect of the tradition into which we are baptized; it is the church's book. As such, the Bible is a sacred book addressed primarily to believers, but the book and the church cannot be separated. It is not a book for individuals to read and interpret as they will. As Saint Hilary of Poitiers said in the fifth century, "Scripture is not in the reading, but in the understanding," and it is only within the church and using its norm of the ancient creeds that Scripture can be adequately understood or rightly interpreted. It is the responsibility of fundamental theology to engage in this activity and provide the community with the fundamentals of its tradition, stated in terms that can be comprehended in a particular time and place in history.

Constructive Theology: Sometimes known as systematic theology, constructive theology operates on a second level of reflection and discourse, providing the church with an intellectual interpretation of its tradition as it is expressed in its fundamental theology. As such, constructive theology helps to make sense of life in our day in the light of the church's tradition. A constructive theology, such as John MacQuarrie's *Systematic Theology* (published by Scribners'), explores systematically what it means for Christians to say "I believe . . ." in a particular time and place. The Christian tradition expressed in the creeds and grounded in God's Word needs to be understood in terms of particular historical, social, and cultural settings. The Christian tradition needs to be appropriated and critically reinterpreted afresh in every generation so that it might answer the questions raised in its cultural setting as well as integrate and illumine the dimensions of modern experience.

Practical Theology: While fundamental theology rationally reflects on what it means to say Jesus is Lord and constructive theology rationally reflects on how this makes sense in a particular social, historical, and cultural setting, practical theology rationally reflects on what it means to live as a Christian in our day. It continually moves back and forth between our life experience and the church's fundamental and constructive theology.

Practical theology is comprised of five dimensions and while each is distinguishable, none is to be understood as separate from the others. Indeed, they are each to be integrated with the others, for properly understood each is simply one doorway into a single whole. These five interrelated dimensions of practical theology are the liturgical, moral, spiritual, pastoral, and catechetical dimensions.

The *liturgical dimension* focuses on life in a worshiping community; that is, the community's cultic or ritual life, which includes all those repetitive symbolic actions expressive of the community's myth or sacred story. The *moral dimension* focuses on life in an acting community; that is, the community's ethical norms and how believers in Jesus Christ and members of his church make decisions in particular moral situations, including our personal decisions in the political, social, and economic realms of life. The *spiritual dimension* focuses on life in a praying community; that is, life in the Spirit or how we are to live in relationship with God, including various acts of devotion. The *pastoral dimension* focuses on life in a caring community; that is, life in service or how we are to live in relationship with our neighbors, which includes those healing, sustaining, guiding, and reconciling ministries that express themselves in care for the sick, the needy, the poor, the hungry, the lonely, and the captive. The *catechetical dimension* focuses on life in a learning community; that is, formation or the processes by which we are initiated into the church and its tradition, and reflection on experience, which also includes the converting and nurturing processes by which we are aided to live into our baptism by making the church's faith more living, conscious, and active, by deepening our relationship to God, and by realizing our vocation, including reflection on experience.

Each of these dimensions of practical theology is related to and includes each of the others. The Sunday liturgy of the church combines spiritual, pastoral, moral, and catechetical actions. The first part of the liturgy, the service of the Word, is intended as a catechetical action. The prayers are a spiritual action, as is the reception of the sacrament. The reconciliation offered by confession and absolution, the kiss of peace, and (when it is offered) the healing provided in anointing are pastoral actions. The moral is addressed as the liturgy frames character and conscience and prepares the people to go forth to love and serve the Lord.

The spiritual dimension of practical theology includes liturgically not only participation in the Eucharist, but the daily liturgy of the hours; it pastorally offers the rite of reconciliation, it catechetically provides for spiritual direction, and it morally aids in discerning the will of God.

The pastoral dimension of practical theology includes liturgically the act of anointing for healing, spiritually the discernment of the gifts of the Spirit, morally the prayers of intercession, and catechetically the preparing of persons to use their gifts and graces.

The moral dimension of practical theology includes: liturgically, the act of baptism that establishes our identity and character; pastorally, the freeing of people to act in healthy ways; spiritually, providing persons with that relationship with God that is foundational to all moral action; and catechetically, helping persons learn to make moral decisions.

The catechetical, which is the focus of this book, also relates to all the other dimensions of practical theology. It therefore cannot be understood as a special field of knowledge, ministerial discipline, or separate activity in the life of the church.

I suspect this three-fold division of theology, and the five integrated dimensions of practical theology, is a somewhat new idea even to many seminary graduates. That can be easily explained. In our modern historical period, practical theology ceased to exist. Its five dimensions broke apart and were dispersed throughout the theological curriculum. To some, liturgical theology became preaching; to others, merely techniques for conducting worship; and among still others, only an aspect of church history. Even in those schools that keep the study of liturgics (typically understood as the history, theology, and practice of worship and/or preaching) in the curriculum, those who taught theory did not teach practice. Separate specialists in liturgies and homiletics were trained and professional organizations and journals to support these specialized fields of knowledge and skill emerged. Pastoral theology became counseling and was typically modeled after secular psychology. The separate field of pastoral care and counseling developed its own training program and certification system known as C.P.E. (Clinical Pastoral Education). It trained its own specialists, offered its own degrees, had its own faculty, professional associations, and journals. Catechetical theology became religious or Christian education and modeled itself after secular pedagogy. It too developed its own degree program, the M.R.E., and a group of specialists, directors of religious education. The field even developed its own schools to train lay Christian educators. Along with this field of specialized knowledge and skills came the usual graduate programs, degrees, faculty, professional associations, and journals. Ascetical theology or spirituality was ignored in most seminaries and within those in which it remained spirituality was turned into either technique or a course or two in the area of historical theology. Moral theology was subsumed under systematic theology, creating a new field of theology and ethics. Finally another specialty was added. While it has had various names, its focus was organization and administration. Concerned primarily with institutional survival, it included church management, evangelism understood as church growth, stewardship understood as church finance, and so forth.

Thus ministerial studies, a conglomerate of subdepartments and specialties, came into existence. More significant, perhaps, is the fact that these studies tended to focus on how-to concerns or the application of what was taught in those areas of study—biblical, historical, theological, and ethical—that were considered more important. And each of these was parenthetically separate from the others and had its own professional associations, journals, degree program, and faculty. Thus a devastating separation erupted between theory and practice. Worse, ministerial studies tended to become devoid of theological foundations as well as spiritual and moral dimensions.

Regrettably, denominations and local congregations modeled themselves along similar lines, established organizational structures to correspond to these divisions of labor, and sometimes hired ordained ministers or professional lay persons to direct or engage in these specialized ministries. Hence, now we have committees for worship, education, pastoral care, evangelism, stewardship, administration, buildings and grounds, and social action in most parishes. Seminaries are organized, faculty hired, and a curriculum provided that models this estrangement of specialized areas of knowledge and skill. Is it any wonder that the church lacks vitality, wholeness of life, and faithfulness of mission and ministry? It is my contention that, until we can reestablish the field of practical theology and equip both the laity and the clergy to engage in this integrating enterprise, the church will be devoid of an adequate means for being a responsive and responsible community of faith.

As a corrective to this modern problem I have written this book. As such, its intention is two-fold. First, to offer an introduction to practical theology by focusing on its catechetical dimension as it is related to the liturgical, moral, spiritual, and pastoral aspects of ministry. And second, to focus this effort on an understanding of stewardship as a useful theological perspective from which to reflect on our communal life in church and society in the light of the Christian story.

Chapter Two

Remembering Who We Are –Stewards of God: Catechetics

Each day the world tells us who we are and how we are to live. Depending upon whom we listen to we are: physical beings who are to make ourselves sexually attractive; intellectual beings who are to accumulate knowledge; consumers who are to acquire material possessions; workers who are to produce products; or pleasure seekers who are to gratify privatized needs. The list could go on. But who are we?

From a Christian perspective the answer is simple, though not easily understood. We are baptized! We have been drowned and brought back to life, we have been adopted into a family—the church—we have been given the name Christian, we have been signed with the cross and claimed as Christ's own forever. We have been re-created in the image of God. We are saints. We are persons of worth. We are lovable, loved, and capable of loving. We are partners with God, stewards of God's creation, entrusted with the Good News of God's saving work in Jesus Christ.

Baptism defines human existence and tells us who we are and how we are to live our lives in a responsive relationship with the holy and undivided Trinity, as reborn sons and daughters of God, Father, Son, and Holy Spirit.

The Episcopal Church has directed that baptism be celebrated most appropriately on a Sunday or other feast, and has recommended that whenever possible baptisms be reserved for one or more of five occasions during the church year, with the catechetical aim of helping us to understand who we are and how we are to live. Other denominations as well are increasingly tending to celebrate baptism as part of the regular Sunday worship, thus making it an occasion for participation by the entire faith community.

These five recommended occasions are: *The Easter Vigil*: We are remade human beings who have died to sin and been reborn to eternal life as witnesses to salvation. *Pentecost*: We are given God's Spirit so that we may discern and manifest God's will and gifts. *All Saints' Day*: We are saints called to realize our potential so that all people will realize theirs. *The Baptism of Our Lord*: We are sons and daughters of God called to minister to the needs of all people so that they will know the blessings of God's love. *Visitation of the Bishop*: We are brothers and sisters who have been adopted into the church to live a communal life as a sign of God's reign in human history.

Thus our baptism establishes our identity as redeemed, creatures in the image of God free to affirm or deny who and whose we are. We are called to live into our baptism, that is, to become who we already are, partners with God in God's plan of salvation for all humanity and all creation. We sin when we deliberately do otherwise, that is, when we squander our inheritance.

In the baptismal liturgy we pledge our love and loyalty to God: Father, Son, and Holy Spirit, the holy and undivided Trinity, who creates, redeems, and perfects all life. We further promise to continue in the apostles' teaching and fellowship, in the breaking of bread and the prayers; to persevere in resisting evil and when we fall into sin to repent and return; to proclaim by word and example the Good News in Christ; to seek and serve Christ in all persons, loving our neighbor as ourselves; and to strive for justice and peace among all people.

In this covenant God bestows upon us mercy and grace and in response we promise to be accountable as partners with God in revealing God's grace and mercy to the whole world. Thus, at our baptism, and each time we renew our baptismal covenant, we reaffirm through vows of loyalty and obligation our lives as God's stewards. And in return, God aids us to fulfill our covenant.

The church's understanding of stewardship is rooted in our baptismal covenant, a covenant in which we promise to be the sacrament of God, the manifestation of God's grace, as a grateful response to God's gift of salvation. At our baptism we are made Christians and incorporated into the body of Christ that we might be led by the Spirit to manifest God's will. God's will is that we be fruitful trustees of God's gifts and graces. Stewardship, properly understood, provides a context for believers in Jesus Christ and members of his church to establish a link between what they believe and how they live. Stewardship is nothing less than a complete lifestyle, a total accountability and responsibility before God. Stewardship is what we do after we say we believe, that is, after we give our love, loyalty, and trust to God, from whom each and every aspect of our lives comes as a gift. As members of God's household, we are subject to God's economy or stewardship, that is, God's plan to reconcile the whole world and bring creation to its proper end.

Thus our stewardship is multidimensional: it includes stewardship as worship, that is, praise and thanksgiving to the one to whom we have pledged love and loyalty; stewardship as proclamation in word and deed, that is, how we act toward the natural world and all humanity, especially those denied God's gifts, the poor, hungry, and dispossessed; stewardship as the acquisition and use of our wealth and possessions for the benefit of all peoples; stewardship as the recognition and use of our talents and skills in the service of others; stewardship as the nonviolent use of power on behalf of justice and peace; stewardship as support for the work of the church; and stewardship as the nature of our common life in the church, including the style of our institutional life, the establishment of priorities and programs, and the use of the church's material and human resources.

Catechetics as a dimension of practical theology strives to answer the question: How do we make God's saving activity known, living, conscious, and active in the lives of persons and the church? In responding to that question, catechetics aims to establish ways to transmit, sustain, and deepen a Christian perception of life and our lives; to aid us to live individually and corporately in a conscious responsive relationship to God; and to enable us to acknowledge and actualize our human potential for perfected personal and communal life. Thus, stewardship is at the very heart of our catechetical ministry. Indeed, catechetics bears the responsibility of making it clear that we are God's trustees. Our theology of baptism clearly tells us that we are stewards of God's grace and called to be fruitful trustees of that which is intended for all humanity.

God's Trustees

Our identity as baptized believers in Jesus Christ and members of his church is related to God's sovereignty. God is the maker and sustainer of all things, ruler over all peoples and nations, the judge before whom we are all held accountable. God is working out God's purposes in history and nothing will ultimately frustrate God's design. We humans are only one aspect of God's creation. While we share in God's Spirit and we are created in God's image, we possess nothing, since all that we are and all that we have belongs to God. God is the sole creator and owner of the universe. We are simply the ones to whom God has entrusted God's affairs, God's property, God's creation. As Paul reminded Timothy: "We brought nothing into the world and we can take nothing out of it" (1 Tim. 6:7).

Since we tend to talk about *our* money, *our* abilities, *our* lives, *our* possessions, it is easy to forget that ultimate ownership rests with God and all are gifts to be used for God's purposes. We are accountable to God for all of life and nothing less than a total commitment to God will suffice. As the author of John's letter put it, "If a person who is rich in this world's goods sees that one of his brothers is in need, but closes his heart to him, how could the love of God be living in him?" (1 John 3:17). How we manage that with which we have been entrusted is at the heart of faithfulness. "Don't delude yourself into thinking God can be cheated: where a man sows, there he reaps," (Gal. 6:7) writes Paul to the Galatian community.

In a world in which what we buy and own determines our self-image and social status, we become increasingly a narcissistic, hedonistic people. For many, life is understood in terms of performance and reward. In its most crass form, this conviction teaches that we get what we deserve, and therefore good people prosper and evil people suffer. People are valued for their usefulness (what they do) and for their economic worth (what they have). High value, therefore, is placed on individualism, competition, competence, achievement, success, consumption, and possessiveness. Thus we have become a people more concerned with having than being.

As Erich Fromm pointed out in his book *To Have or to Be* (published by Bantam), the difference between being and having is the difference between a society built around persons and one fixated upon things. Because the society in which we live is devoted to acquiring and consuming more and more, we rarely see any evidence of the "being" mode of existence and most people see the "having" mode as the most natural, and even the only acceptable, way of life.

While many will acknowledge that who they are, what they have accomplished, and even what they have earned is not entirely of their own doing, few are willing to attribute these to God. Instead they explain that their intelligence was inherited from their parents, and it was just fate that they were born into an affluent family in an affluent society. They trace the bread they eat to a shopkeeper, a baker, a farmer, and ultimately to the earth, though they make clear that it is the money they have earned from their labor that puts this bread on their table.

Still, most of us who have grown up in the church have the sense of a bigger picture and are at least perfunctorily grateful to God for these apparent givens of life. But we have a problem at a deeper level: while acknowledging these as gifts from God, we tend to emphasize what our role has been and thereby become selfish and possessive about the products of our labor. We thank God, but then act as if they are ours to do with as we please.

Most of us are in favor of making good and faithful use of our intelligence and abilities in the service of God: we favor the responsible use of time and talent; we favor the maintenance of healthy bodies; we favor the gracious and responsible use of our material possessions—our houses, cars, books, and clothes. But most of us are not as clear about our money. We work hard for it. As a good friend put it, "To acquire my income, my family has had to pay a big price, and so have I. Sometimes all I could give them were things —very good things, no doubt, like quality health care, but still things. We enjoy living comfortably though I have no investments. Our family doesn't take lavish vacations or buy expensive clothes or even go out to eat often. I must admit we have never worried about a meal, a roof over our heads, or a bill for that matter. While I'll share most everything I have with anyone and everyone, I must admit that I still act as if the money I have earned is mine."

Money in our sort of society may well be the central issue for stewardship. As soon as anyone in the church talks about money, a lot of people get uneasy. Indeed, more heated feelings are aroused over money than over doctrine.

The church, the body of Christ, is to be the sacrament of God, that is, an outward and visible sign of inward and spiritual grace or a visible material sign of an invisible spiritual reality. This body of Christ comes together to perform symbolic acts that are intended both to express and to shape the life of the body during the week. The discipline of regular participation in the Sunday Eucharist symbolically relates to our understanding of the nature, purpose, and meaning of time. The discipline of proportionate financial giving through the weekly offering symbolically relates to our understanding of the nature, purpose, and meaning of money. A financial pledge is like a rule of life, like the discipline of prayer. It is not an end in itself, but a means to an end. Similarly, the intention of the act is as important as the act itself.

Recall Jesus saying, "Where your treasure is, there is your heart also" (Matt. 8:21). It is true, of course. That is why the stewardship of money, in a society in which a money economy provides the basis upon which we live, is such an important symbol for our whole life. Our interests have a habit of ending up where we place our investments. Our material lives are important because they determine, as well as express, our spiritual lives. It is simply misleading to work on the assumption that if people are committed, they will give and therefore to place our emphasis on seeking commitment. It is wiser to work on the assumption that if people give, they will become committed. We are more likely to act our way into a new way of thinking than to think our way into a new way of acting. Behavior comes before belief. We live as Christians in order to come to the faith of Christians. Thus did Jesus spiritualize the economic aspects of material life. Irenaeus, the early church father, wrote, "Our Lord instructed his disciples to offer to God the first fruits of his own creation not as though he had need of them, but that they themselves might not be unfaithful or ungrateful."

The Economics of Christians

The Reverend Peter Lee is my colleague, friend, and rector. He is one of the most faithful, competent priests I know. It is my privilege to serve with him as a priest associate in the Chapel of the Cross in Chapel Hill, North Carolina. As my priest, he is not only pastor to me, but on many occasions teacher as well. One day we were discussing parish life and he commented that Archbishop William Temple called Christianity the "most materialistic of the world's religions." We are an incarnational people, he continued, who experience ultimate truth in human form. It should be no surprise, therefore, that our faith demands a response in concrete, specific, material terms.

The constant temptation of the church is to overspiritualize its message. The notion that the Lord of the Universe was actually present in human life, in human flesh, experiencing human pain and death, was so objectionable to some in the early centuries that numerous alternative understandings emerged. But each of these overly spiritual, otherworldly understandings was labeled heresy.

The same heresy (a truth run wild, a truth that denies other truths) is still present today among those who say that the church is spiritual and does not need institutional existence, buildings, or budgets. Such a view eventually leads to the conviction that Christianity has little to do with our real lives. On the contrary, the Christian faith teaches an incarnate Christ and calls for a response that is the offering of our selves, our souls and bodies. "That is why,"

Peter Lee explains, "we teach that the discipline of giving is the duty and measure of our fidelity. What we give of our money is the clearest sign of what we give of our lives. As Christians we give because we have been given to. We are the recipients of a lavish love. Giving is at the heart of Christian life. Our need to give is more than a duty, more than a response to need, it is a sign of our understanding of what life is about." I have also always been impressed that no matter what date the vestry chooses for stewardship Sunday, Peter Lee always preaches on the assigned lessons, for he is wisely convinced that if any sermon on stewardship is to be faithful, it has to be true to the Word of God proclaimed by Scripture and experienced by the church.

I have never heard Peter Lee discuss the details of our parish budget or try to sell the congregation on our parish program. He has always been more interested in our human need to pledge a significant portion of our material wealth as part of a sign of our commitment to the sovereignty of God over all of our lives and a witness to what we say we believe. Stewardship in our parish has never been seen as a tip to God for services rendered or a matter of paying our bills.

I recall the story Peter Lee once told. When he was in college during the business recession of 1958, his father wrote him to suggest that since family income had been reduced, he should apply for a scholarship. There was no consideration, he pointed out, of his father cutting his tithe to the church, for he considered that a priority, a witness that came first in their family's life, a duty that was welcomed and assumed because it expressed a relationship to God and to the community of faith, the family of God shared by all of them.

The Christian faith has a deep and abiding concern for economic life. We humans are economic beings. The societies we develop are comprised of economic systems. The churches we were baptized into are economic institutions. And the state of the economy is one significant measure of the quality of human life. The Christian faith necessarily expresses itself in economic terms and the church, the embodiment of that faith, is necessarily concerned with the economic aspects of our individual and social lives. The church's sacred Scriptures are infused with economic concerns: the care of the earth, just commercial relationships, and responsibility for the poor.

While there may be no particular Christian way to manage the economy, Christians must continually make economic decisions on our national budget—on the proportion of military spending to social welfare, for instance. We cannot avoid issues of economic justice, such as the distribution of food, shelter, fuel, and health care in the United States and, indeed, throughout the world. Christians must not only act on behalf of the economic needs of those in their midst but, through denominational programs and government agencies, on behalf of economic needs they can never adequately or justly address alone.

Christian faith is concerned with economic life, indeed, with every aspect of life. However, while we are obliged to live faithful economic lives, no particular economic system is Christian. All economic systems stand under the judgment of God. Capitalism, communism, or socialism is each to be affirmed or condemned to the extent that it orders a society so that justice is done, all persons are cared for equally, and abundant life for each and every person is achieved. All economic systems are only a means and never an end in and of themselves. We are to seek first God's kingdom and use whatever economic system appears most faithful in our historical, social, and cultural setting.

We live in a world characterized by accelerating industrialization, rapid population growth, increasing poverty, widespread hunger and malnutrition, the depletion of nonrenewable resources, the pollution of the environment, and increasing military preparedness. The gap between rich and poor grows wider. A few consume what belongs to all. Individualism, nationalism, and isolationism flourish.

In face of an increasingly interdependent world, people are more and more choosing to retreat to privatized religious experience and life, while the government and national agencies pass on their responsibilities to those least able to manage them in our complex social order. Frightened by the present and moved by self-interest, people engage in reactionary thinking and acting.

Faithful Stewardship

Stewardship typically has been turned into a yearly campaign for funds and an attempt to get people to devote their service to the church by teaching in the church school, singing in the choir, being on the vestry, or assisting in the liturgy. A yearly pledge of time, talent, and money, based upon programmatic budgetary needs to run an institution, is a strange understanding of stewardship. How will we ever recapture an understanding of stewardship that calls us to be a sign and witness to God's promises? As stewards of God, we are invited to join God's action, God's mission in the world. We are Christ's body, God's sacrament, so that God can be present in human life and history. It is for this purpose that God calls us into the church.

We are stewards, managers, administrators of a trust. We can arrange, manipulate, employ, develop, but God owns the title. We are to so manage our personal and corporate trust that it will benefit all humanity, now and in the future.

We are not to manipulate for our own benefit or glorification. We are to manage life in the interest of accomplishing God's will. When we pray "thy kingdom come, thy will be done" we acknowledge the priority of God's will. The more we are given, the more will be expected of us. We need not feel guilty for having food so long as the energy we receive from it is devoted to concerns such as the elimination of hunger.

All that we have—our lives, intelligence, sensibilities, abilities, potential for growth, opportunities in every moment of time, blessings of the earth and inheritance—are gifts from God, given to us for the benefit of all God's children. Stewardship begins with a recognition that God is the generous giver from whom we have received all that we have. It is the gifts of God that establish us as the people of God, as the stewards of God's gifts intended for all God's children. We are to be responsive and responsible people. In the words of Saint Peter, "Each one of you has received a special grace, so, like good stewards responsible for all these different graces of God, put yourself at the service of others . . . so that in everything God may receive the glory, through Jesus Christ, since to him alone belongs all glory and power forever and ever. Amen" (1 Pet. 4:10–11).

As a baptized people, we are to acknowledge life, salvation, possessions, power, influence, knowledge, and abilities as trusts from God. We are to seek to develop them and then discern God's will for their use so that we might be faithful to these trusts as stewards with God in the shaping of the world's future. God has chosen to work through us and with us that God's will might be done and God's reign come.

Stewardship expresses our continuous response to the grace of God through responsible daily life. The church is a community of stewards aware that the responsible management of God's affairs has been entrusted to all people. Christian faith, therefore, affirms both the sacred and the secular, the spiritual and the material. That is the point of the incarnation and the truth of sacrament. The spiritual is always and only known through the material and the material is only truly perceived when we affirm its unity with the spiritual. Secular humanism is only a heresy when it denies the sacred spiritual aspects of life. Correspondingly, sacred spiritualism becomes a heresy when it denies the secular humanistic aspects of life. The physical and material aspects of life are to be affirmed. Healthy Christian faith is not an escape into the spiritual. The faith of the church is expressed in an ancient blessing used at the Eucharist. As the bread and wine are presented, the priest says "Blessed are you, Lord God of all creation, you give us this bread and wine to offer, gifts of creation and work of human hands, they will become for us the bread of life and the cup of salvation."

Human life is healthy when the sacred and the secular are in harmony. In a secular age the secular consumes too much importance, but in a sacred age the opposite occurs. The secular, with its concerns for the material world (for social, political, economic life) and for the rational aspects of human activity, is as important to Christian life as is the sacred, with its concerns for the spiritual world (for transcendent life) and for the nonrational (intuitive) aspects of human activity. The doctrine of the incarnation, rightly understood, holds them together. As we enter what I believe is the genesis of a new sacred age with its rightful concern for the sacred and transcendent dimensions of life, I fear we will lose the value of the secular and humanistic dimension of human existence. A healthy understanding of stewardship demands that the human and the divine, the sacred and the secular, the spiritual and the material, the transcendent and humanistic, piety and politics be united.

Stewardship, like human nature, is communal. Men and women created to reflect God's nature and live in personal relationship with God and neighbors are given the responsibility of maintaining and managing the whole of creation. God is the holy and undivided Trinity. God lives in community and we, created in God's image, are meant to live in community as well. As a community of faith, we are God's representative on earth charged both to reveal who

God is and to care for God's world. We are not independent entrepreneurs free to live for ourselves alone.

As I write these words it is Trinity Sunday. After I celebrated the Eucharist at the Chapel of the Cross in Chapel Hill, North Carolina, I returned to my typewriter with the thought that stewardship means among other things that we are commissioned to share in the work of the holy and undivided Trinity: One God, Father, Son, and Holy Spirit, creator, redeemer, and perfecter of all individual and corporate life. That conviction concerning God implies that we are to take part in the creation and preservation of all life; it implies that we are to set all captives free and to act on behalf of the rights of all peoples until justice and equality is achieved and all live in abundance; it implies that we are to stand as witnesses for and with those who need an advocate until all creation is perfected and the peace and unity of all peoples is realized.

The strangeness of God is God's promise to be with and for us always. Nothing can separate us from this loving presence. God promises that God's reign has come, is coming, and will come, that all creation is intended to be reconciled, that every creature is to live securely, in harmony and community with every other creature, and to work toward the joy and well-being of every other creature. It is a vision that encompasses all reality, a vision of salvation, the holiness and wholeness of all creation.

Christian Faith, Revelation, and Vocation

As in every age, we address the catechetical issues of faith, revelation, and vocation from within a particular historical, social, and cultural context. Of course, our understanding of that context is influenced by our personal experience of it, yet we share a great deal.

Briefly, I sense that our shared experience is that we live in a period of radical transition. For a long time we have been dominated by a secular, scientific, materialistic society in which religious pluralism has produced a relativism and skepticism devoid of historical consciousness and futuristic vision.

Our world is one of contradictions and shifting perceptions: while searching for community, we celebrate a rugged individualism; while longing for being, we advocate having; while desiring a this-worldly relevance for human life, we live for an otherworldly salvation; while wishing for a spiritual reality we can know directly by participation and encounter, we acknowledge solely a material reality known only indirectly by sense experience and reason; while affirming a humanitarian commitment, we support an inhuman social order; while confessing belief in the Gospel, we live as if God has not acted in Jesus Christ to transform human life and history; while defending both the intellectual and intuitional modes of consciousness, we have been both anti-intellectual and anti-intuitional; while confessing a commitment to prophetic judgment and change, we have acted on behalf of conservative institutional and national survival; while conscious of our expanded human choices and seemingly unlimited possibilities, we have become immobilized and escapist; while aware that we are called to be a sign and an advocate of a new world, we have blessed the status quo; while possessing great personal and social resources, we have acted as if we were miserable worms without influence; and while our rhetoric speaks of paradox and integration, we live lives of disintegration, flip-flopping from one heretical extreme to another. Amid these confusions, we are confronted by a world that is radically changing before our very eyes. Within the context of this challenging reality, I would like to reflect on Christian faith, revelation, and vocation as they relate to the catechetical ministry of the church.

The Christian faith provides us with a particular way to understand our lives and history, makes particular experiences possible, and implies particular ways of living. Christian faith or perception can best be expressed in the language of poetry and story, and the symbolic narrative at the opening of the following Eucharistic prayer offers one version:

God of all power, ruler of the universe, you are worthy of glory and praise.

At your command all things came to be: the vast expanse of the interstellar space, galaxies, suns, the planets in their courses, and this fragile earth, our island home.

From the primal elements you brought forth the human race, formed us in your image, and blessed us with memory, vision, reason, imagination, sensitivity, and skill.

You gave the whole world into our care so that with you, our Creator, we might govern and serve all your creation. But we keep turning against you and each other betraying your trust. Still you did not abandon us but again and again you call us into covenant with you. Through prophets, sages and priests, you reveal to us your will and teach us to hope and work for your rule of salvation.

In the fullness of time you, in your love, came to our aid in Jesus Christ, born of a woman, and transformed all human life and history, opening to us the way of justice and peace, freedom and equity, community and human well-being. Living as one of us, but without sin, he preached the good news of salvation to the broken, freedom to the captive, joy to the sorrowful, and new life to the dying. To fulfill your purpose he gave himself to death and in your raising him from the dead you destroyed the power of evil and gave the whole creation new life.

And that we might live as you intended you sent your Holy Spirit to continue your work in the world to achieve sanctification and bring salvation to all.

Therefore we praise you, joining the heavenly chorus together with prophets, apostles, and martyrs and with all who in every generation have looked to you in hope to proclaim your glory. . . . [3]

At our baptism we are made Christians, incorporated into this story and vision, and bound to an ever-renewable covenant, in which we promise:

> To devote ourselves to the apostles' instruction and the communal life, to the breaking of bread and the prayers.
> To persevere in resisting the power of cosmic, social and personal evil and whenever we fall into sin to repent and return to the Lord.
> To proclaim by example and word the Good News of God in Christ.
> To seek to serve Christ in all persons, loving our neighbors as ourselves.
> And to strive for justice and peace among all people, respecting the dignity of every human being.[4]

The central vision of world history in the Holy Scriptures is that all creation is in unity and harmony, every person living in interdependence and security and working toward the joy and well-being of all others and of nature as a whole. It is a vision of a social, political, economic world in which all people in their uniqueness are drawn into community around the will of God, that is, the care and maintenance of all of God's creation. It is a vision encompassing all of reality under God's governance.

God acted historically to produce this world and subsequently acts in history to develop it according to God's visionary plan. Humanity is created by God in God's image to enter into community with God, self, neighbor, and the natural world, and to actualize God's vision through creative acts. Still, we experience ourselves as broken and incomplete, we experience one another as fragmented and distorted, we experience our world as torn and twisted. We share with all humanity longings for freedom and community, but they appear beyond our grasp. It is easy to conclude that human nature is fundamentally evil and/or that we are slaves to cosmic and social evil.

The Christian faith proclaims that this experienced existential slavery and alienation has been overcome. While it has not yet been eliminated—the battle between good and evil within each of us and the world continues—a dramatic change has occurred and life can be different.

Through Jesus Christ, God has overcome personal and social disorder and reestablished the possibility of creation's intention. It is a mystery, of course—not in the sense of something that we do not understand, but in the sense of something that continually surprises us by bringing into being that which had appeared impossible.

Through the mystery of this historic event we are placed in a new relationship to God, self, neighbor, and nature, we are called to a new self-understanding, and we are granted the possibility of a new style of life. By the grace of God we are justified, that is, we are given a new life, and we are empowered to be sanctified, that is, to actualize our new possibility for human personhood.

Baptism is the sacrament of justification: it announces our new human condition and possibility. The Eucharist is the sacrament of sanctification: it nourishes and nurtures us as we live into our redeemed human condition, the persons we were created to be and indeed already are. As such, we are liberated historical beings in process, actualizing through God's help our true humanity by moving from a distant past toward a hidden future of reconciliation with God, self, neighbor, and the natural world.

Humanity experiences both a life of essence—who we truly are by God's grace—and existence—who we are as we live our lives day by day. Christian faith brings us to a vantage point from which we can grasp our authentic life, and Christian revelation, as the experience of new life lived in relationship to God, aids us in the fulfillment of our vocation to make and keep human life genuinely human.

Further, a new age has dawned, a new creation has been given birth, a transformed order has been established. God is sovereign over the world and human affairs. God has changed both the direction of history and the human condition so that God's long-standing historical purposes might come to completion and God's work, begun with the creation of the universe, might reach fulfillment.

No matter how problematic or obscure it might be, history is purposeful, directional, and intentional. We are not alone; God, the power of unmerited love, is with us, liberating and reconciling all of creation. God is in love with humanity, offering to us not what we deserve, but what we need. The purpose of human life is to respond to God's love and join God in God's history making.

While most of our human efforts go badly and even our accomplishments appear inadequate, we can have hope, for God transforms every failure and death into success and new life. God is at work in the world. The plan of God is moving irresistibly forward. We can dream the impossible dream, envision the wildest hope and be confident. Nothing can ultimately stand in the way of God's plan.

There is no need to live in fear or to amass material possessions, power, or prestige. We can trust and risk living in freedom. Indeed, we can sing and dance in the face of evil, for we know that good will ultimately triumph.

In spite of the evening news, we can have peace and unity within the human family. Humankind can live together in justice, friendship, abundance, and tranquillity. This will not be achieved without struggle and disappointment, however. We cannot afford an evolutionary optimism or naive sense of natural progress. The path to the actualization of God's reign, like the human spiritual pilgrimage, will be difficult and filled with setbacks. All we can know is that history will end, not when or by what series of events. The kingdom of God is in our midst and yet hidden in the future. We are called to do the planting and leave the harvest to God.

The revelation or experience of salvation through God's grace confirms our fundamental goodness. Broken, incomplete, fragmented, distorted, twisted, and torn though we and our world appear, our true condition is whole health, well-being, unity. "Jerusalem is built as a city that is at unity with itself" (Ps. 122:3). We are now capable of becoming who we already are. No longer is a gloomy pessimism appropriate. Neither is a naive optimism, but the battle is won and good will eventually, by the action of God, triumph.

The victory that Christ reveals is both the goodness of God and the goodness of humankind, created in the image and likeness of God. Just as the victory of Christ was not easily won, we continue to wrestle with our tendency to sin as we open ourselves to God's transforming power to become what God intends.

Religious experience or revelation is the necessary and natural outcome of Christian faith, just as any interior meeting with God precedes any exterior expression of Christ's life or vocation. For Christian faith, God is the Good News that human community is possible. Christian faith leads us to a sacramental understanding of human life, and it brings persons into a redemptive encounter and a living relationship with God. While Christian faith transforms our consciousness, revelation transforms our personal and social lives, making us aware and desirous of living as God intends and has made possible. Divine revelation, when experienced by us existentially, transforms our relationships to God, self, neighbor, and nature; it reveals to us the possibility of a new way of life. God's revelation re-creates us. The Good News is that God is always present to human life and creatively involved in human history, bringing about the conditions by which we might fulfill our true humanity. Thus in the solitary silences of human experience we hear "the still small voice." It is not an echo of our own thoughts and impressions, but the experience of the redemptive encounter with God calling us to fulfill our potential for wholeness of life with God.

We are twice born, once in our natural birth and then again at our baptism. At our baptism we celebrate the truth that God has reached into the heart of our being, transformed us, and empowered us to live a life of grace. Through our baptism we die and are reborn, we receive the gift of God's sanctifying Spirit, we are made saints, we are called to ministry, and we are incorporated into the body of Christ. So radically altered are we that we can never again think of ourselves as merely natural persons. A permanent change has been announced and reenacted. Our vocation is to live into our baptism, to become fully in community who we already are.

Christian vocation can be characterized individually and corporately as life with God under the lordship of Christ. It is life in the world but not of it, participating in ordinary activities in the social, political, and economic contexts of human community to the end that God's will is done and God's reign comes. It is not longing for another world or another place in history. At its deepest level, our Christian vocation is simply human life devoted to helping to make and keep all human life genuinely human.

Christian vocation is not simply the fulfillment of "religious duties" such as saying prayer, the support of the church, reading the Bible, and the like. It is rather to be the agent through which God realizes God's intentions for creation. Our vocation is to actively participate in a witnessing community, the church. Our vocation is to be an advocate and sign of God's rule, to become a historical agency through which God is remaking the human world.

We are called to identify with others, especially those who are denied God's intention for all humanity, to become vulnerable to the world's suffering, to serve human need, to bring liberation and reconciliation to those who suffer from oppression and estrangement and thereby to make disciples, that is, to call others to recognize their new human condition and God's intentions for life.

Christian existence must always be understood as life within

community and social-political-economic history. Christian vocation assumes a radical community centeredness, the acceptance of
ethical norms, and the search for faithful decision in the light of the
complexities of human individual and social life. It further assumes
that we will engage corporately in acts that witness to God's will.

The church is to be a sign and an advocate of this new reality so
that all humanity might know what God has made possible for
those who have the eyes of faith to see and the will to live accordingly. Thereby is the church the body of Christ, a hidden, prophetic creature of God's Spirit, an instrument of God's transforming power, and a witness to God's continuing revelation in history.

It is one church, a paradox to the mind: sinful yet holy; imma-
nent yet transcendent; divided yet one; continuously in need of reform yet the bearer of God's transforming eternal word; a human
institution and a holy community; a desperate assembly of baptized
sinners living, sometimes unconsciously, by grace yet also an intentional, obedient, steadfast, faithful company of converted, visible
saints; a mystery even to itself, but aware, in often incomprehensi-
ble ways, that it has a mission in the world and a ministry both to
those who by birth or decision find themselves, not entirely by
choice, within it and to those who stand outside it.

The church's mission, like Christ's, is to live in and for the Gospel,
to witness in word and deed to these perceptions and experiences.
Christianity from the beginning has been essentially a missionary
community: the Gospel has been committed to the church and the
responsibility of the church is to be a living sign and an advocate of
this Gospel. As such, the church is to be an ambassador of Christ
and the Gospel, to be of service to all people so that individual and
corporate life might be more truly human and enriching. The
church is to be the sacrament of God: an outward and visible sign of
an inward and spiritual reality.

In our life in the church, catechetics focuses on faith, revelation, and vocation. Stewardship as it relates to faith is concerned with our inevitable, spontaneous response to God's grace as expressed in the life, death, and resurrection of Jesus Christ. The Christian is a steward of the Good News of God in Christ. Along with other Christians, we share the responsibility of sharing this Gospel with others. It is required of us that we be found faithful in manifesting God's Word for the world.

Stewardship as it relates to revelation is concerned with the practical expression of our relationship with God. Jesus made clear to his disciples that God is sovereign and we are responsible to God. The Christian revelation denies that we are autonomous, independent individuals, for we do not even own our own lives. We are placed in the world through God's sovereign freedom, we are maintained in life and health through God's sustaining goodness, and we are truly ourselves when we live a dependent life in relationship to God by submitting to God's will, which is our true happiness.

Stewardship as it relates to vocation is concerned with the devotion of our lives and resources to the purposes of God. As stewards, we must render an account to God of the way we use our time. To use time for the glory of God is to use it in the making of life rather than in the making of a living. As stewards, we must render an account of the way we use our abilities. To lay our abilities on the altar of the service of God is to dedicate their powers to the service of humanity. As stewards, we must render an account of the way we use our possessions. All progress in the spiritual life waits upon our willingness to make Christ the Lord of our possessions and to render unto God a faithful stewardship of all material reality. Catechetics embodies the nature and aims of stewardship. Catechesis provides us with insight into the process by which we achieve these catechetical aims.

Chapter Three

Living into Our Baptism: Catechesis

Baptism tells us who and whose we are. Baptism calls us to a life of stewardship. As believers in Jesus Christ and members of his church, God has made a covenant with us to be stewards of God's spiritual grace, God's unearned and unmerited love through visible material signs. God has called us to be God's sacrament, God's presence and activity in human history so that the world when it looks at how we live our lives within the church will see a sign of God's purpose for human life, and when it looks at how the church acts in society will see a sign of God's will for human life being manifested in history.

Our baptism provides us with a picture of who we really are and a picture of the world as God intends it to be. Throughout our lives we are to strive to live into that baptism. Herb Brokering, a Lutheran pastor friend, tells of visiting a Lutheran church near the Mexican border. When he arrived he was told that Israel (his parents were Mexican) was to be baptized. Crossing the border to find a present for Israel, he fell in love with a pair of sandals. But they were for an adult, and Israel was an infant. He tried to explain his

37

problem to the saleswoman, but she said it didn't matter, Israel could grow into them. Israel slept through the ceremony but his parents seemed to understand; baptism was a pilgrimage. A few months later he returned to learn that Lisa, Israel's cousin, was to be baptized. Back across the border he went in search of another present. This time he fell in love with a pair of booties only to learn they were for a two-month-old and Lisa was ten months old. He once again tried to explain the situation to the saleswoman, but she said that it wouldn't matter, for Lisa could hang them on the wall to remind her of her baptism. At last he really understood baptism; it was living between booties and sandals, between remembering and growing into, and all of us are on a pilgrimage with Lisa and Israel.

Catechesis is the process by which we prepare persons for their baptism and the process by which we aid persons to live into their baptism.

In *The Book of Occasional Services* (published by the Church Hymnal Corporation) there is a rite for the Preparation of Adults for Holy Baptism that is similar to the Rite of Christian Initiation of Adults used in the Roman Catholic Church. Both the Roman and Episcopal churches have acknowledged the normative nature of mature adult baptism and Christian initiation. *Normative* means "standard," rather than "normal" or "typical," for in both traditions infant baptism continues to be affirmed and encouraged for the children of the faithful. However, by making mature adult baptism normative, a number of important theological and catechetical convictions are communicated.

First, Christian initiation involves both God's action and a human response. God acts first: grace is prevenient, never acquired or earned by a human effort; and while there are numerous appropriate ways for a person to respond over a lifetime, ultimately a mature, rational, moral response to God's ever-present love is normative. Commenting upon 1 Cor. 11:27, Regis Duffy in his book

Real Presence writes, "St. Paul warns us that our sacraments and worship cannot be divorced from our lives. If the religious symbols we participate in express commitment to the Gospel vision of love and service but our lives remain unchanged, then something is radically wrong."[5]

Second, baptism is a sacrament and not magic. A sacrament is an outward and visible sign of an inward and spiritual reality; it does not make something true, it only makes that which is already true real. The sacraments are not encounters that "give grace" but opportunities for people already in God's grace to celebrate that fact.[6] Baptism is not something we must do in order to convince God to give us salvation, it is what we do because we already know God's salvation. A child does not need to be baptized to acquire God's grace or be saved. Baptism is not a magical act that makes God do something for someone that God would not do without that act.

And third, adult baptism asserts the importance of mature faith and life. While baptism makes known to us what is true, it assumes that we must always be living into, or realizing, its truth. Augustine in one of his homilies comments that when the priest presents the bread at the Eucharist and says "The Body of Christ," he says in effect: "Be what you see. Receive who you are."[7] To respond "Amen" is to affirm convictions that necessitate a lifetime to actualize. Thus baptism is the beginning of a journey for both infants and adults.

However, by continuing to affirm infant baptism as a legitimate and laudatory exception to the standard, the church also teaches three other important truths about baptism. First, it establishes the fact that we are communal beings. Our faith is always first someone else's faith. We come to the church not primarily because we have faith, but because we want it. In the admission to the catechumenate in *The Book of Occasional Services* the priest asks, "What do you seek?" and the catechumen replies, "Life in Christ"; life in the body of Christ, the church, the community of faith. No one can be a Christian alone. Secondly, it is the faith of the church that legitimizes any baptism, whether the baptized is an adult or infant. For the church to baptize, to adopt people into the community, it needs to examine and reform its life as a faithful community. And third, a human being is always in process, that is, on a lifelong pilgrimage of daily conversions and nurture. Both transformation and formation are continuous aspects of human life. Catechesis and evangelization are related. Our end is the wholeness of humanity. To reach this end, the church must be in a continual state of reform and renewal: that is, of opening of ourselves to God so that our visions and actions might be reshaped again and again. Evangelization is that process within the church that effects a new consciousness which the process of catechesis aids us to incorporate into our faith and life.[8] The faith of the church is one that calls for repentance, a continuous and lifelong process of conversions. It is not only the little wicket gate through which John Bunyan's pilgrim quickly passes as he abandons the City of Destruction but the entire pilgrimage to the Celestial City. Baptism is something we grow into as we are continuously converted day by day at ever-deeper levels of our personality by the means of the Word of God. Conversion proceeds layer by layer, relationship by relationship, here a little there a little, until the whole personality has been re-created by God. Infant baptism makes clear this necessary lifelong process of living into our baptism, which includes evangelization and catechesis.

In the new rubrics for catechesis in the *Episcopal Rite for the Christian Initiation of Adults* we also have some standards or norms established for the process of catechesis. Let me describe this recommended procedure and then draw out the implied principles.

Stage one is a precatechumenal period of inquiry, a time for evangelization. It suggests an informal, natural setting in which lay persons share their life stories and what it has meant in their daily lives to have been baptized as a believer in Jesus Christ and made a member of his church. It is a time for inquirers to also share their life stories and reveal what they are seeking. In a context of honest discussion, the Christian faith as a way of life in community will emerge. More important, an effort is to be made to help the inquirer to see where God's grace has been present in her or his life and how Christian faith and life in the church can help to make sense of this experience as well as give life meaning and direction. If any inquirers appear to desire "life in Christ," the priest (pastor) needs to help them examine and test their motives in order that they may freely commit themselves to pursue the lengthy, disciplined process of preparation necessary before baptism. If inquirers are deemed ready, a sponsor must be chosen from among the most faithful in the community to accompany them on their pilgrimage.

The next period, known as the catechumenate, begins with a public liturgical act at a Sunday Eucharist. At this time the catechumens and their sponsors begin a process that includes the following elements: First, the catechumens are to choose a ministry in which to engage. This ministry is not intended to be a service to the church, such as singing in the choir, but a ministry in the world such as service to the poor, hungry, sick, neglected, needy, or infirm. Second, with their sponsors they are to attend regularly the Sunday liturgy and explore how the story of their lives and the story of salvation celebrated in the liturgy intersect. Third, they are to gather regularly with their sponsors to develop experientially a spiritual discipline for their lives that includes learning to pray, meditate on Scripture, and discern God's will. During this period the candidates will be regularly examined and prayed for at Sunday liturgy. When it appears that a catechumen is ready she or he is enrolled as a candidate for baptism (if the baptism is to be at the Vigil of Easter, this occurs on the first Sunday in Lent; if it is to be at the Feast of our Lord's Baptism, then it occurs on the first Sunday in Advent). During this period, amidst a number of important liturgical events, the candidates are encouraged to examine their consciences and to participate in the rite of reconciliation; to fast, meditate on Scripture, and pray in the context of directed retreats to test if they are spiritually and emotionally prepared. They are also to reflect theologically on the Christian faith and life in which they have been participating during this period of preparation. This important rational reflection on their experiences in the church provides an opportunity to reflect on Scripture and explore the church's fundamental theology and ethical norms to the end that they will understand and be able to defend what Christians believe and how they are to live.

Then comes baptism (which properly incorporates baptism, confirmation, and Eucharist in a single rite of initiation and parenthetically establishes the standard of a single initiation rite for all those baptized, no matter what the age, as well as the standard of baptism as a covenant to be renewed over and over again in appropriate ways throughout one's life). However, the process is not over. Following baptism the newly baptized enter a final stage of catechesis. During the season of Eastertide or Epiphany they are helped to experience and reflect on the fullness of communal life in the church as a witnessing community in the world as well as gain a deeper understanding of the meaning of the sacraments: baptism and Eucharist, the two great sacraments, and anointing, reconciliation, marriage, ordination and confirmation, the other lesser sacraments. Thus the newly baptized learns that his or her growth and development have just begun and must continue throughout his or her life in the church.

Principles for Catechesis

From this recommended process a number of principles for catechesis can be established: First, the process of catechesis is always a converting and nurturing process. It is concerned with a conserving need to form or shape persons in the tradition of the church and a transforming need to liberate persons from erroneous understandings and ways of life. Catechesis is misunderstood as solely a conservative activity. While its first concern is the acquisition of the church's story and vision (tradition), it takes seriously our human experience and the lives we live out of our own story and vision. Because it assumes that both our lives and the community's understanding of Scripture and tradition must always be tested by reason and life experience, it also establishes a process for a dialogue between them, but always within the context of a faith community.[9]

Second, the process of catechesis is one of experience, reflection, and action. We experience before we make sense. We cannot understand what we have not first experienced. *Orthopraxis* (right behavior) comes before *orthodoxy* (right belief). It is *lex orandi* (rule of worship) that leads to *lex credendi* (rule of believing). We act our way into thinking. This is the truth that justifies an infant's participation in the Lord's Supper. And it rightfully encourages the church to provide an environment where children and adults can experience the Gospel, participating with others in living that Gospel in community and witnessing to it in the world.

Third, the process of catechesis is related to readiness and not time, to appropriateness and not a packaged program. Different persons have different learning needs, different learning styles, and different capacities for learning. Catechesis must be tailored to meet human need and potential, rather than trying to fit persons into pre-established programs and organizations. Persons learn at different rates and bring their own varied experience with them. Readiness is the key, not the completion of a particular course of study.

Fourth, the end of catechesis is a life-style that includes our total being as thinking, feeling, willing persons. It is not solely a concern, as some would have it, for believing certain doctrines (whether understood or not), for having particular religious experiences, or for willing to be a Presbyterian, Episcopalian, or United Methodist, etc. A Christian life-style includes *character*, a sense of who we are and the necessary dispositions, attitudes, and values related to that identity; *conscience*, an activity of the whole person making rational decisions as a believer in Jesus Christ and a member of his church as to what is a faithful act; and *conduct*, a life that others see as a sign and witness to the sovereignty of God.

Fifth, catechesis is a personal pilgrimage with companions. It is not a process of molding individuals into some predetermined design nor is it a process of simply aiding persons to grow up according to some internal design. That is, it is not doing things to or for persons. It is, rather, a process of journeying with another person in community, of sharing life together over a route we travel. It is doing something with others. It presupposes a searcher, a person who is willing to let his or her life be a resource for the other, and the conviction that truth is revealed to both of them as they share in this mutual pilgrimage quest.

In my earlier works I spoke of faith development and four stages of faith. While I do not negate the insights expressed at that time, I have moved on to what I believe to be a more adequate way to describe our spiritual pilgrimage. Now, I prefer to speak of three pathways or trails to God. Each trail leads to God; none is superior to the others. While the first path is a natural place to begin and therefore appears appropriate for children, each may be traveled at any time, in any order. Similarly, we may return to any trail at will and the third trail is, interestingly, one that combines the first two; indeed, something is missed if we limit ourselves to one trail, yet each still reaches the same goal or summit.

The first path I have named the *Affiliative-Experiencing Way*. On this slow, easy path the community focuses its concern on the passing on of its story and thereby framing its identity and that of its people. Together they seek to participate in experiences of life in a family-like, caring, nurturing community. Intuitive knowledge—which is nurtured by participation in the arts and expressed through symbols, myths, and rituals—is desired. The authority of the community is trusted as together they aim to establish a sense of tradition. As they journey along, they are dependent on others for guidance and help as they learn what it means to be a pilgrim.

The second path I have named the *Illuminative-Reflective Way*. On this somewhat difficult traversing over the rocks, the community encourages persons to search for alternatives, as there is no marked trail. In these individual efforts to make it over the cliffs, persons discover the meaning of community, of trust, and of intimacy. The community supports persons as they begin to assume responsibility for their own faith and life. Together they quest after intellectual knowledge, which is nurtured by rational reflection on their experience (theology) and is expressed through signs, concepts, and reflective actions. The authority of the community is thereby tested by experience and reason as they seek to live prophetically in a visionary world. As they journey along together, persons are encouraged to establish a sense of their independence and are urged to explore their own way, sharing their discoveries with the community.

The third path I have named the *Unitive-Integrating Way*. On this complex path the community encourages persons to move back and forth between the two previous ways and thereby create a new way. On this path persons are aided to discern what they should live for and give their life to, and they are provided opportunity to assume responsibility for community life. Now persons combine intellectual and intuitive ways of knowing and find meaning in both contemplation and action; they seek to reconcile the paradox of Catholic substance and its conserving of the tradition with a Protestant (Reformed) spirit of prophetic judgment and retraditioning. No longer caught between believing that there is *the* truth that some authority knows and believing that there is *no* truth, which means people can believe what they like, they become aware of pluralism's options, accept a truth for their lives and, while advocating it, are open to other possibilities. Within the community they seek to live an interdependent, apostolic life and find that they are able to both affirm and aid those traveling on the other two paths.

Obviously the community needs to provide guides and companions for each of these ways.

Sixth, catechesis asserts that this process is an activity of the whole community. Catechesis assumes a communal understanding of human nature and the necessity of a faithful community; that is, a community that shares a consciousness of a common memory and vision, a community aware of its roots and committed to its vision of the future. Catechesis assumes a community with a common authority, which for Episcopalians since the 1968 Lambeth Conference includes Scripture, tradition, and reason (reflection on experience). It also assumes common rituals or repetitive symbolic actions expressive of the community's memory and vision, which for Episcopalians is established in the 1979 *Book of Common Prayer* and *The Book of Occasional Services*.

And last, catechesis assumes a particular sort of common life together that is like that of a family. As such, it is a faith family that focuses on every aspect of life: the religious, political, economic, and social; it calls for the elimination of role playing and the involvement of the total personality; it is never neutral to emotion, but involves life shared in the depths of joy and sorrow, pain and pleasure; it is a life regulated implicitly by custom and hence does not demand explicit bylaws; it is a community in which our obligations to each other include whatever love demands rather than a contract in which if the community does not act as I believe it should, I leave; and last it is a community in which our worth is not in what we contribute or how much we participate, but is a consequence of our being. Each of us is of value, for each of us is in the image of God. None is of greater worth or value than any other.

Further implications should be obvious. We need to examine our common life and become more critical of every aspect of parish life. We need to establish the degree to which our life is an expression of culture and the degree to which it is faithful to the Gospel. We need to contemplate whether or not we have interpreted the Gospel through a cultural perceptual field or whether the Gospel is providing us with a perceptual field necessary to transform the culture in which we live. Since catechesis includes both processes of intentional enculturation and rational reflection, both experience and reflection must be taken seriously. In order for catechesis to be faithful, the church needs to be a moral community of mature Christians seeking to provide for themselves and those they adopt into the family, a context in which the Gospel is experienced and reflected upon; that is, an ever-reforming, nurturing, caring community of faith and life.

Thus, catechetics and catechesis address the ends and means of believing, being, and behaving in community. Understood best as a communal interactive process, catechesis can be defined as deliberate, systematic, and sustained interpersonal helping relationships of acknowledged value that aid persons within a faith community to know God, live in relationship to God, and act with God in the world.

Catechesis aims to provide persons with a communal context for living into their baptism. This context is an environment for experiencing the ever-converting and nurturing presence of Christ as day by day, in community, Christians gather in the Lord's name to be confronted by God's Word, respond to the gift of faith, pray for the world and church, share God's peace, present the offerings and oblations of their life and labor, make thanksgiving for God's grace, break bread and share the gifts of God, and are thereby nourished to love and serve the Lord. Catechesis aims to provide persons with a context for falling in love with Christ and thereby having their eyes and ears opened to perceive and hence experience personally the Gospel of God's kingdom; it further aims to provide a context for persons to live in a growing and developing relationship with Christ that they might be a sign of God's kingdom come; and last, it aims to provide a context for persons to reflect and act with Christ on behalf of God's kingdom coming.

The Church as a Human Community

The church is a pilgrim community of memory and vision. The vocation of the church is to hear God speak, to see God act, and to witness in word and deed to these experiences. Christianity from the beginning has been essentially a missionary community to whom the Gospel has been committed. The responsibility of being a living sign of and witness to that Gospel is the vocation of every Christian. Christians, as ambassadors of Christ and the Gospel, are to be of service to all people so that individual and corporate life might be more truly human and enriching.

Catechesis implies, therefore, the need for (1) a knowledge and understanding of the church's living tradition, including its ethical norms and the reflective cognitive abilities to use that tradition in responsible moral decision making, (2) a deepened authentic piety, unifying attitudes, affections, sensibilities, motivations, commitments, and values into an exemplary style of communal life, and (3) a clear vision of God's will for individual and corporate human life with concomitant skills for its realization. Thereby, believing, being, and behaving are united in the lives of persons who in community have a relationship to Christ and a commitment to the Gospel.

Catechesis is a ministry of the Word in which the faith is proclaimed and interpreted in verbal and nonverbal ways for the formation and transformation of persons who are to be understood as communal beings in a lifelong quest to live in a love relationship with God and neighbor. It is a ministry of the Word in which persons are converted religiously, intellectually, and morally as well as initiated into the communal life of the church, and nurtured and nourished in its particular and peculiar perceptions, understandings, and ways of life. Catechesis occurs within a community of faith where persons strive to be Christian together. It aims to enable the faith community to live under the judgment and inspiration of the Gospel to the end that God's will is done and God's community comes. It unites all deliberate, systematic, and sustained efforts to discover the will of God, to evaluate the community's interior and exterior life, and to equip the community for and stimulate it to greater faithfulness. Catechesis is concerned with both continuity (conserving an authoritative tradition) and change (making a prophetic judgment on its understanding of that tradition). It is a process intended to both recall and reconstruct the church's tradition so that it might become conscious and active in the lives of maturing persons in community. It is the process by which persons learn to know, internalize, and apply the Gospel in daily individual and corporate life. As such, catechesis aims to enable the faithful to meet the twofold responsibility that Christian faith asks of them: community with God and neighbor.

Catechesis, therefore, is a life's work shared by all those who are called to participate in the mission and ministry of the Christian church. It values the interaction of faithing souls in community, striving to be faithful in-but-not-of-the-world as a transformer of culture. The fundamental question that catechesis asks is this: What is it to be Christian together in community and in the world? To answer this question is to understand the means by which we *become* Christian within a community of faith. Catechesis, therefore, intends to help us understand the implications of Christian faith for life and our lives, to critically evaluate every aspect of our individual and corporate understandings and ways, and to become equipped for and inspired to faithful activity in church and society.

Importantly, catechesis acknowledges that we are enculturated or socialized within a community of memory and vision. Baptism incorporates us into a family with a story, a living tradition. This adoption into the church creates a change intrinsic to the self. We are historical beings, implicitly and explicitly influenced and formed by the communities in which we live and grow. Catechesis acknowledges this influence and challenges the community to be morally responsible for the ways in which it influences the lives of others. While catechesis affirms that persons are both determined and free, the products of nurture and the agents of nurture, it makes it incumbent upon the community of faith to accept responsibility for disciplined, intentional, faithful, obedient life together. This makes socialization not a process to be undergone passively, but an activity in which persons interact with the culture, each influencing the other in multiple ways. The differentiation some have drawn between socialization and education in terms of process is inadequate. Perhaps the real difference is in an understanding of the learner. The language of education tends to perceive the learner as an individual who associates with others and forms institutions. The language of socialization tends to perceive the learner as a communal being whose identity and growth can only be understood in terms of life in a community that shares a common memory, vision, authority, rituals, and familylike life together.

When we ask, What is the content we are going to make available? and, What we are going to do with it? are we not asking if it is possible to be a Christian and believe whatever one wishes or interpret the community's tradition in any way one pleases? Is not the answer to both no? We live in a wasteland of relativity where individuals believe they can write their own creeds and interpret Scrip-

ture any way they like. Catholicism's concern for an ordered authority may lead to tyranny, or the denial of the reality of individual insight; Protestantism's concern for freedom may lead to anarchy, or
the denial of the reality of communal wisdom.

Saint Vincent of Lérins wrote: "We must hold what has been believed everywhere, always, and by all." The Creeds are at once the
criteria and the norm for believing and behaving.

A Christian teacher is not free to teach or encourage private
opinions, but only to propagate and defend "the faith that was delivered to the saints." The modern mind stands under the judgment of the kerygma. We are to bend our thoughts to the mental
habits of the apostolic message, for "repentance" means a "change
of mind."

Catechesis, Culture and Transformation

Catechesis, understood as the process of enculturation, has been
misunderstood as a singularly conservative process aimed at the
shaping of another's life by a tyrannical authority. Catechesis, however, is a process that aims at avoiding the relativistic, existential
educational processes that easily fall prey to anarchical freedom. It
has been misunderstood as unconcerned about persons; however, it
does aim to avoid the trap of individualism so prevalent in our culture. It properly aims at leading persons to radical reorientations in
their perceptions, experiences, and lives. It witnesses to the Lordship of Christ, to the Good News of God's new possibility, and to
the Gospel's prophetic protest against all false religiousness so that
the church will not lose its soul and become an institution of cultural continuity maintaining the status quo, rather than an institution of cultural change living in and for God's kingdom. Catechesis
seeks to provide the means by which the church might continually
transform its life and the lives of its people into a body of commit-

ted believers, willing to give anything and everything to the cause of historically mediating God's reconciling love in the world.

Christian faith does run counter to many ordinary understandings and ways of life. It is hardly possible for anything less than a converted, disciplined body to be the historical agent of God's work in the world. Conversions are a necessary aspect of every developing mature Christian's faith. The church can no longer surrender to the illusion that child nurture, in and of itself, can or will rekindle the fire of Christian faith either in persons or in the church. We have expected too much of nurture. We can nurture persons into institutional religion, but not into mature Christian faith and life. The Christian faith and life by their very natures demand transformations. We do not gradually educate persons by stages to be Christian. To be Christian is to be baptized into the community of the faithful, but to be mature Christians is to be continually converted and nurtured in the Gospel tradition within a living community of Christian faith.

Authentic Christian life is personal and social life lived on behalf of God's reign in the political, social, economic world. One cannot be nurtured into such life—not in this world. Every culture (and institution, including the church) strives to socialize persons to live in harmony with life as it is. The culture calls upon its religious institutions to bless the status quo and it calls upon religion's educational institutions to nurture persons into an acceptance of life as it is.

But God calls the people of God to be signs of *shalom*, the vanguard of God's kingdom, a community of cultural change. To live in the conviction that such countercultural life is our Christian vocation, in-but-not-of-the-world, necessitates conversions as well as nurture.

Who but the converted can adequately nurture? And who but the nurtured can be adequately prepared for the radicalness of transformed life? Catechesis focuses, therefore, on both formation, the growth of persons, and transformation, the change of persons within a community of faith. Catechesis proclaims and explains the Gospel so that faith might be made conscious, living, and active. Catechesis as intentional enculturation is, therefore, a ministry producing continual reform and growth. Thus, catechetics, as one important dimension of practical theology, seeks to integrate liturgical, ascetical, moral, and pastoral aspects of the church's life with the church's authoritative tradition.

Catechesis as enculturation rightly focuses on how people's patterns of meaning and style of life are acquired. Enculturation describes that dialectical process involving an interaction between the world in which we live and the world of the self over a lifetime. This process includes both intentional and unintentional influences that transmit and sustain a people's learned, shared understandings and ways of life.

Enculturation, however, is not a determinative process of indoctrination, nor is it solely a conserving one. Persons bring both their inherited personality and free wills to each interaction, thereby being not only influenced but influencing. While each of us is our history, each of us also makes history. In every moment of time we are free to accept or reject the processes of formation that surround us and attempt to shape us. Further, a people's learned, shared understandings and ways are both continuous and changing. A culture dies if it does not both maintain roots in the past and engage in change on behalf of a future vision.

Enculturation is not a process solely concerned with children; it is lifelong. We are always being shaped by and shaping the culture in which we live. In a rapidly changing culture such as our own the young significantly engage in the enculturation of adults. Christian catechesis, understood as enculturation, is a lifelong mutual process. Catechesis needs to be both a nurturing and a converting interplay of all generations in community from birth to death. Each of us is born into a society whose members practice a way of life—a culture. These shared, learned understandings and ways of life are transmitted to each new generation in part by their peers, but especially by the adults in their lives. Children pay attention to the world around them and their encounter with this world is important to their growth and development. In all societies, nature and nurture conspire together to shape the child into the understandings and ways of his or her culture. Thus, patterns of perceptions, meanings, attitudes, values, and behaviors are shaped early. A child responds to the world in ways adults indicate as appropriate; the expectations of adults are soon internalized. Some examples may be useful.

In Java a child's first recognizable word is typically *njuwum*, "I humbly beg for it." By five or six a Javanese child has an extensive repertoire of graceful words and actions. The language we learn orients us toward interpersonal relations or problem solving, having or being, giving or receiving.

How we relate to others is shaped early. In Japanese culture a child is inclined to see nonkin as kinlike. For the Japanese child the world of people is made up predominantly of kinfolk, real or pseudo. It is natural later, therefore, for the Japanese adult to perceive the corporation as a family. Whether or not we envision ourselves as living in an interdependent world is shaped in early years.

Little children of the Chippewa Indians, before they can eat, are sent with a dish of food to a neighbor so they will learn to give and share. If a family has a successful hunt, rather than store the meat the children are sent around the village to invite everyone else over to come get some of it.

In the United States most children are brought up with an obligation to play and have fun. Little is asked or expected of children, except perhaps to take care of their own room and cooperate with essential personal routines such as eating, sleeping, dressing, and toileting. But in Nigeria small children are given major responsibilities for the welfare of the group. They are nurtured to see the enduring gratification of working well and responsibly at a congenial task. Work is seen as enjoyment in Nigerian culture, but in our North American fun culture work is the drudgery you have to engage in to earn enough money to play.

We often complain in the United States of the strong influence that the peer group plays during adolescence. It need not be so. In Amish culture, children identify with adults and not the peer group. This is also true among Soviet children, Mexican children, and many others. We bring up our children with a sense of individuality and self-reliance, we shape them to perceive the world as always and necessarily changing, and we create a child-centered society where children are encouraged to form peer-group friends and relationships. Is it any wonder that adults have less influence on children's lives?

There is no need for more examples, but it is important to note that every aspect of life related to an understanding of stewardship is being shaped during childhood, usually unconsciously and unintentionally. It is also being sustained and deepened in adult lives in a similar manner. The ends for which we live, the means by which we live, our dispositions and attitudes, our understandings of the meaning and purpose of life and our lives, our convictions concerning right behavior and proper conduct are all being acquired, sustained, and deepened throughout our lifetime. We are being shaped and we are shaping others. Regrettably, we are not always aware that this is occurring or what is being learned. Catechesis rightfully includes both formal instructional processes and informal, unstructured, and spontaneous formation processes.[10] However, it is the latter that are typically ignored, which explains why I have chosen to place my emphasis here.

Robert Ellsberg of *Sojourners* magazine recently interviewed

Robert Coles, the well-known child psychiatrist. Coles commented on the enormous discrepancy between the teachings of the Bible on justice and fairness and our lives, which are often expressive of exploitation, greed, competition, and individualism. Coles went on to explain that the Christian values of community and equality are not easy to hold up when we are interested in perpetuating a privileged situation. If we take Christianity seriously, he said, it is a radical and indeed scandalous religion.

Ellsberg then asked, "How do we bring up our children as Christians?" Coles answered by pointing to the stories of Flannery O'Connor, many of which take place on a battlefield of belief and doubt in which the antagonists are children trying to hold on to a sense of the spiritual amidst adults who know only the material. O'Connor, he pointed out, is trying to show what is necessary for an earnest inquiry into the meaning and purpose of life. She saw what the Bible was getting at. In all her stories she confronts the self-satisfied with Christian radicalism.

And then Coles pointed to a story he shared in *The Privileged Ones* (*Children of Crisis*, vol. 5, published by Little, Brown) concerning a child who grew up in a very rich Florida family. This child's experiences in the church affected him and prompted him as a child of eleven to talk about the teachings of Christ in school. This upset his teachers and fellow students. He kept telling them how awfully hard it would be for rich people like his family to get into heaven and that the poor would inherit God's moral and spiritual kingdom. Ultimately this boy ended up in psychotherapy because everyone believed he had a problem and needed help. His parents were told to stop taking him to church. The sad ending is that he eventually lost those Christian perspectives and became another entrepreneur. [11]

If we are to be stewards of God, our lives in the church will need to provide us with experiences and opportunities for rational reflection that encourage us to confront concretely, not abstractly, our lives inside and outside the church. A proper understanding of catechesis provides us with a model for doing just this and thereby provides us with the insight we need to faithfully live into our baptism and to become faithful stewards of God.

Chapter Four

Life as Eucharist: Liturgical Catechesis

It was a family Eucharist and I was celebrant. A mother, father, and their seven-year-old son had come forward to receive communion. In my tradition if you wish to commune, you hold up your hands, if you wish a blessing instead, you cross your arms over your chest. The mother and father knelt at the altar rail, closed their eyes, bowed their heads, and held up their hands. Their son stood erect, looked me in the eyes, crossed his arms, but held them extended toward me. I stopped and looked at him. "Do you want to eat or do you want a blessing?" I asked. "I'm hungry," he answered. "Here," I said, "this is the body of Christ, the bread of heaven. There is enough for everyone and since you are hungry have all you can eat." I put a piece of bread in each of his hands. His parents looked up aghast and following the service I found them waiting for me in the rear of the nave. They explained that they were angry and wanted to talk. I answered, "Fine, I will be happy to hear why you are angry if you are willing to listen to why I am not angry." They agreed and we went off to talk. They were angry about many things. Their list included anger at children being in church rather than church school (they said it made it impossible for them to worship), children receiving communion before they were confirmed (they said that they didn't want their son to commune until he was much older because he didn't understand what he was doing), and they said that I had destroyed the spiritual meaning of communion by putting bread in both their son's hands (they didn't think I should have even talked to their son). My response went something like this:

Children belong in church. Eucharist is a family thanksgiving banquet, not an occasion for privatized adult meditation. Church school is good for adults who need to rationally reflect on their experience of Christian faith and life, but children need to experience the Gospel and there is no better way to do so than by participating in the community's liturgy. And if they do participate, how can we explain to them that, although they have been baptized and have become members of Christ's family, they nevertheless cannot eat with us?

I explained that there were two ways to know. One way was an intellectual way of objective reflection and the other was an intuitive way of subjective experience. This second way was natural for children, just as it also was necessary for adults. We all must experience reality before we can make sense of it. Further, this intuitive way of knowing, nurtured by the arts, was best expressed through symbols, myths, and rituals. Children need to have the experience of communion before they can rationally understand it. If these parents wanted their child to understand the Lord's Supper they would encourage him to share in the meal.

And last, I tried to explain that I had a lot of extra consecrated bread and I was concerned about what their son might have concluded if he, being hungry, had to remain so while I, already overweight, consumed the bread that was left instead of sharing it.

To this day I am troubled by that encounter. I was never able to help those parents understand my point of view because their experience of worship for thirty years had been so different. The Eucharist as life and life as Eucharist had eluded them and so instead of their seeing my action as an example of the faithful stewardship of God's grace, they saw it as a distortion of their religious convictions.

Our lives are a gift. We are stewards to whom the responsible management of our lives, God's gift, is entrusted. As faithful stewards, we are to live a Eucharistic life—at least, that is what the church's liturgy is intended to teach us. Stewardship is to be the daily manifestation of a continuous response to the grace of God freely given in the sacrament of the Eucharist; thereby worship and work are connected.

The worship of God is not an escape from the world or the responsibilities of daily life. Liturgy encompasses every activity of God's people; it properly includes both our daily life and our cultic life, that is, our ritual life or those repetitive symbolic actions expressive of our community's memory and vision. Insofar as we separate our cultic and daily lives, we live in an unhealthy state, for the two are intended to be integrated. A change in one should produce a change in the other. That explains why those who are content with their lives do not want their rituals changed and why those whose lives have changed are always in search of new rituals to support them. That also explains why throughout history when the church discerned that it was not being as faithful as it ought to be, it sought to reform its cultic life. And that explains why in the early church persons wishing to prepare for baptism into the church's community life were required to give up participation in the culture's secular rituals, the public athletic events. Communal religious rituals are intended to express and shape our understandings and ways of life. The way we worship is to be the way we live.

If there is any ritual act that is specifically and essentially Christian it is the celebration of the Eucharist; its purpose is to shape us and empower us to live eucharistic lives. If that is not occurring, we had better seek to discover the inadequacy of our rituals. If a life of stewardship is not being manifested in the lives of Christians who regularly participate in the Eucharist, then the way we celebrate this ritual may need to be reformed.

Godfrey Diekmann, the Roman Catholic liturgical scholar, tells of an address given by the late Bishop Spuelbeck of East Germany at a preparatory commission on liturgy of the Second Vatican Council. Amidst debate on the radical reform being recommended for the Roman rites, especially the Sunday Mass, the bishop from Meissen reminded the commission that the communists had their own pseudoliturgies and that all Roman Catholic societies and schools had been eliminated; only the Sunday Mass remained. He begged the commission to be as radical as possible about the revisions of the rite so that it could become the basis for a common identity, the basis for shared faith, hope, and love, the basis for a courageous witness in the world.[12]

During the past decade mainstream Protestant and Roman Catholic liturgical scholars have reached substantial agreement on the nature and character of the church's worship. Having concluded that the reform and renewal of the church's life and witness were essential for faithfulness in our day, they set out to reshape the church's worship. All looked to the early church for insight. And so while maintaining their historic denominational identities, all reached similar conclusions. Thus the new Roman Rites, the Episcopal *Book of Common Prayer*, the Presbyterian *Worship Book*, the Lutheran *Book of Worship*, the trial rites of the United Methodist Church and the United Church of Christ (and others) are amazingly similar and in intention virtually identical. Let us take a moment to reflect on these numerous reforms, with special attention to the issue of life as God's faithful stewards.

A Reshaped Liturgy

For a long time it was typical of worship for many Christians to celebrate morning prayer each Sunday or the Service of the Word segment of the complete Eucharistic Rite, making the sermon of central importance. In its extreme form some focused the act of worship solely on a forty-five-minute sermon with the addition of a few hymns, a pastoral prayer, and a lesson from Scripture. In this activity, the clergy, typically identified as professional ministers possessing special knowledge and skills, were, perhaps along with a choir, the dominant actors. Other Christians typically celebrated the sacrament of Holy Communion and either trivialized or eliminated the sermon. In its extreme form amidst the saying of their own prayers, some focused solely on witnessing the mysterious transformation of the bread and wine into the body and blood of Christ. In this activity, the clergy, typically identified as priests possessing special power, were the dominant actors. Thus it was that half the church functionally took the Word seriously and the other half took the sacrament seriously—both in effect, estranging word and sacrament. As a result, the minds of Christians were formed to separate Word and deed, telling and doing.

In contrast, recall the opening of Mark's account of God's Good News. Jesus, having attracted a number of students, takes them on the Sabbath to a synagogue for class. A number of visitors sit in on his session. His teachings about the presence of God's long-awaited and hoped-for reign of peace and justice, liberation and reconciliation was startling, but what amazed the people most was that Jesus, unlike most teachers, never said, "Do as I say and not as I do." In Jesus they found a teacher who acted as if he really believed what he taught and performed acts to support his words. That is why his teachings had authority and that is why he converted so many to his way of seeing things.

It is well to remember that the fifth book of the New Testament is entitled the Acts of the Apostles and not the Talk of the Apostles. Acts evangelism was normative for the early church. The Gospel the church preached was the Gospel the church lived. It was by show and tell that the church evangelized the world. Folk then as now were attracted to God's Good News because the church taught as Jesus taught, through word *and* deed. Is it any wonder then, that when word and sacrament became separated or when one or the other became dominant that the church's stewardship of the Gospel through faithful evangelization was negatively affected? The renewal of the church's life thereby necessitates the reshaping of its worship. Thus agreement has been reached: the norm for Sunday worship is Word *and* sacrament; the norm for Christian daily life is word and example.

Further, the structure of this rite or the order of worship is also held in common. It now looks like this:

> *Gather in the Lord's Name.* During the penitential season of Lent a general confession and absolution is placed here, while during the season of Eastertide the confession is eliminated entirely so that we might better understand ourselves as a redeemed people.
>
> *Proclaim and Respond to the Word.* While typically numerous lessons from the Scripture, sermon, and creed, these may include various readings, songs, talks, conversations, silence, dances, dramas, intrumental and choral music, and other art forms, but a reading of the Gospel is always included.
>
> *Pray for the World and the Church.* During seasons other than Eastertide and Lent a general confession and absolution follows these prayers.
>
> *Exchange the Peace.* Here or after the breaking of the bread all are to greet each other in the name of the Lord, establishing through this symbolic act that in the church there are no strangers or estranged people.
>
> *Prepare the Table.* Along with the bread and wine (gifts of creation and the work of human hands, which will become the bread of life and our spiritual drink), other offerings and oblations of our lives and labor are placed on the altar table. (The offering is made during the Eucharistic prayer.)
>
> *Make Eucharist.* Following a shared greeting that brings the

community to the table, thanks is given to God for God's work in creation, God's covenant with all humanity, and God's revelation of God's self in history; the community proclaims God's glory in song, gives thanks and praise to God for the salvation of all the world through Jesus Christ, represents Christ's action at his Last Supper, proclaims the mystery of faith, offers its gifts, opens itself to God's sanctifying presence and activity through the Holy Spirit, sings a doxology, and prays the Lord's Prayer.

Break the Bread. The church reenacts Christ's sacrifice of love.

Share the Gifts of God. All the baptized come to share the bread of heaven and the cup of salvation.

And having expressed thanks, the community is *Sent Forth to Love and Serve the Lord.* Within this drama the community shapes its life as stewards of God called to be a sign and witness to God's presence and activity in history, called to proclaim in word and deed the Good News of God in Christ.

A second agreement concerns the unifying principle and content for the community's celebration of Word and sacrament. In the recent past, some Christians have made the words of the Bible their focus. Typically this meant that the preacher would use verses of the Bible as inspiration for the sermon. Some preachers followed suggested readings from a lectionary and some chose their own lessons. Some used the Bible as a point of departure for their message and others used it to proof-text their convictions. Both believed they were being bible-centered. While desiring to focus on Scripture, most of these sermons were either doctrinal (focused on theological content) or moral (focused on specific implications for daily life).

Other Christians made the church year, Advent through Pentecost, the unifying principle and content of the community's celebration. Typically these were the same churches that emphasized the sacrament. Participants usually had to be instructed in the meaning of the church year, for it was used for doctrinal purposes and interpreted from a dogmatic point of view. Perhaps more important, in almost all denominations another calendar emerged to supplement and inform worship in the church. There were the usual national holidays such as the Fourth of July, and secular holidays such as Mother's Day. More important, there was Stewardship Sunday, used for fund raising and the annual pledge canvas, Theological Education Sunday, and a host of other special days to raise money for the church and its mission projects. There also was Christian Education Sunday and rally day for beginning the Sunday school in the fall. The list was endless. Church life became separated from daily life, doctrine became separated from religious experience, and action became separated from belief. The culture became secularized and lost its spiritual foundation; so did the church. The church also became institutionalized (one voluntary association among others) and lost its communal familiar character.

Today we have agreed that the focus of worship is to be the Christian story as it intersects with our human story. The church year and appropriate assigned lessons from the Hebrew Scriptures, the Psalms, the apostolic letters, and the Gospels have been agreed upon as the content for the church's celebration of Word and sacrament. Perhaps more significant is the move toward understanding the church year in terms of story, *the* story that informs, illumines, and transforms our human story.

The church is best understood as a story-formed community, a people on a pilgrimage through time, through seasons of profane time made holy and whole by sacred time. How we date time is significant for how we live from day to day. It makes a difference if we date time by the church's year, the school year, or the fiscal year. It makes a difference if we celebrate baptism days, saints' days, and holy days or birthdays, anniversaries, and state holidays. It makes a difference if our rhythm of life is ordered by the seasons of football and basketball, winter and summer, or Advent and Pentecost. We have agreed that the church year is best understood as related to our human pilgrimage and the Scriptures that inform the seasons of the church year as expressions of our human experience and journey. The aim of liturgy is to so celebrate, live, and tell God's story in community that our human stories, our lives, might be shaped to serve God's purposes and thereby given meaning and health.

The Christian story is centered on Easter, in which we are bold to proclaim, and challenged to live in the light of, God's reign, power, and sovereignty. A new world, a new creation, a new reality, personal and social, has been born, made possible, and ultimately determined. Ordinary time, half of the church year (from Pentecost until Advent) is a season best characterized as "growing old together," as striving to live this Good News, day by day, until we grow weary and the vision fades. Advent, a season characterized by *pregnancy*, is intended to recapture the lost dream. It is a season of anticipation, patient waiting, longing and letting go, giving up control. Christmas, a season characterized by *birth*, celebrates possibilities. Aware of the anxiety possibilities imply, it also celebrates hope. Epiphany, a season characterized by *childhood*, is lived in the imagination; it is a season of naive witness to the possibility of that which appears impossible. Lent, a season characterized by *the adolescent struggle*, makes us aware of the principalities and powers in our lives and world that distort God's dream and our journey to perfection. Then Eastertide, a season characterized as a *honeymoon*, in which we celebrate the dream come true. Ascension follows, a season characterized by *adulthood*, in which we are told that we, the church, are now the body of Christ but impotent. And then the joy of Pentecost, in which we are made potent and are sent forth to live as a sign and witness to God's Good News. Ordinary time follows;

it is a season in which *the* story touches our individual and corporate life stories—shaping, informing, illuminating, and transforming them as we journey in the church as God's chosen people called to so live out God's story that the world's story will be shaped, informed, illuminated, and transformed.

A third agreement concerns our involvement in the liturgy. For a long time persons who attended Sunday worship did so as observers. Some came to hear a good sermon and/or choir while others came to see Jesus at the Mass; in both, the action at the liturgy was dominated by the clergy, as silence, womblike postures (kneeling), and (at best) passive participation dominated the laity's involvement in the liturgy. Since persons express their identity through participation in liturgy and their experience of the liturgy shapes their identity, most persons acquired a highly privatized, individualistic, passive, noninvolved, clericalized piety. Is it any wonder, then, that standing rather than sitting or kneeling, communal participation in prayers, lay leadership in the planning and execution of the liturgy, the kiss of peace, language that everyone could understand and use, regular participation in the communion by all baptized persons regardless of age, increased congregational singing, and fewer choral anthems caused dismay and confusion? Without knowing why, people sensed that their understanding of themselves was changing. A communal understanding of human nature was replacing an individualistic one. Christian life as active participation in the mission and ministry of the church was replacing an understanding of ministry as the responsibility of professionals. Clerical religion has become shared ministry as the body of Christ, the people of God. The sacraments as signs of corporate life in the body of Christ replaced the sacraments as religious products supplied by the clergy. The issue now becomes how is Christ personally present in us as a community living in political, social, economic history rather than how is Christ present in bread and wine. It is because

Christ is present in the community of faith that Christ is also present in the Word and sacrament.

Since the church is the sacrament of God, its function is to so live its life that the whole world will know what is true for it also. We are not to bring people to church to get something they wouldn't have otherwise, but to help them see the grace that has always been present in their lives so that their coming to church will be an act of thanksgiving. As the sacraments make God's grace *real* rather than *true* for us, we come not from fear or duty, but in gratitude. We return in gratitude to share love we have already been given. As a community for others, we witness to the new life that this awareness brings so that others will be able to see the grace that is in their lives and respond accordingly.

One other aspect of this communal participation theme is the affirmation in the new liturgies that we are persons who think in a variety of ways: intuitively through subjective experience and intellectually through objective reflection; that we experience through the use of all our senses: seeing, tasting, touching, smelling, and hearing; and that we act through the use of our wills on behalf of what we discern to be God's will. For a long time many Christians ignored all their senses save hearing, affirmed only intellectual or objective thinking, and understood behavior as particular actions performed out of obedience, fear or duty rather than respect and gratitude. Now it is the whole person, living in relationship with God, self, neighbor, and natural world, as a believer in Jesus Christ and a member of his church discerning and making mindful decisions as to the will of God and acting accordingly.

A fourth agreement concerns our human nature. Since our rituals shape us, most people have come to think of themselves as ultimately no good, miserable worms, sinners. For years a penitential understanding of Christian life has dominated the church's rituals. In the preaching tradition grace was always subservient to sin. We seemed to believe that people had to hear the bad news before they could hear the Good News. In the sacramental tradition a long, somber confession with an emphasis on the belief that there was no health in us dominated the beginning of the liturgy and continued throughout the liturgy as the people acknowledged that they were unworthy through their manifold sins to make any sacrifice, and that they were not worthy so much as to gather crumbs from under God's table. Kneeling at the altar rail, eyes closed and heads bowed, they begged for grace and received enough to make it through another week. It is not difficult to understand why most did not want to celebrate the Lord's Supper very frequently (they explained that it was to make communion more important, but I suspect it was because it was so depressing). Worse, they came to believe that there was little value in what *they* did and little difference they could make in the world.

Now the rites of the church are more celebrative. They are rites of a redeemed community that celebrates its life as a saved people and their potential as daughters and sons of God. Of course they sin, but their sins are a denial of their true being. God in Jesus Christ has made all life new. We humans are to live in and into that reality. Now the only question is why we do not act as a redeemed people.

Add to this the apostolic emphasis of the liturgy and you find a new understanding of mission and stewardship. In the old days at the close of the liturgy the people returned to their wombs, were offered a pietistic and quietistic understanding of God's peace through soft organ music, a benediction, a choral amen, and the long extinguishing of the candles. Now at the close of the liturgy they are sent forth, as a thankful people, to love and serve the Lord, fully aware of what God has done and has empowered them to do. Indeed, in those traditions that have deacons (who are ordained by the community to bring to it the world's denial of justice and peace, and the needs of the oppressed, suffering, sick, and troubled), it is the deacon who gives the final charge, after the community prays (standing) that God will send them out to do the work God has given us to do as faithful witnesses to Christ our Lord. And the people exclaim, "Thanks be to God" and then leave on the exit hymn to do just that. Needless to say, if our lives are shaped for mission and ministry, we will not only see that life is to be lived as a sign and witness to God's Good News of a redeemed humanity and world, but we will gratefully and willingly provide financial support for that mission and ministry.

José Castillo, a Spanish theologian, wrote, "Where there is no justice, there is no Eucharist." Insofar as a sacrament fails to produce appropriate fruits in the lives of participants, the failure is on the human side of our encounter with God in the Eucharistic liturgy. Grace and gratitude are linguistically related, as are *charis* and *eucharistia* in Greek. We receive the self-giving love of God and the test of our thankfulness is manifested in the giving of ourselves and our benefits in the service of others. The Eucharist properly celebrated is a sign of that gracious justice by which God invites the hungry and the thirsty to his table. It is intended to move us to engage in a fair distribution of God's bounty as it is present in our tangible resources.

In the beginning, in Genesis, humanity is given food by God. Food is a gift of God. We are to take it and share it, not hoard it, possess it, or overindulge in it. Having fed us, Jesus calls us to feed others (John 21:15–17): "Feed my sheep," he says; Christ, who feeds us, points us to the hungry. We come to Eucharist aware that we are what we eat. We ponder what it means to eat God; if we come hungry and thirsty for life and are fed with the life-giving presence of Christ's body and blood, then we must ask what it means to go forth and feed all others with our bodies. Thus the Eucharist offers a judgment on our consumer society and its values, a society in which we eat and eat and are never satisfied, a society in which we deny the physically hungry the food they need because we ourselves are not spiritually fed.

It can be otherwise, of course. I recall a Eucharist planned by a group of people one summer at Kanuga, an Episcopal Conference Center in western North Carolina. We gathered in a parking lot and were divided proportionally into the populations of the first, second, and third worlds. On the hood of a car were twenty loaves of bread. When the celebrant arrived he announced that today we represented the first, second, and third worlds but that in Christ there is no East or West. As we sang that hymn with gusto, the bread was divided as the world's bread is divided. Those in the first world ended up with a significant hunk of bread for each person while those in the third world had difficulty making sure that each person had a small piece. The celebrant announced that all of us present lived in this first world and prayed that we might be grateful for our abundance. A multiple "Lord have Mercy" made sense that day. The Gospel was the story of the feeding of the five thousand from John's account of God's Good News. The offering was whatever bread we had been granted. Then as we gathered in groups of fifty on the conference lawn, the Eucharistic prayer was prayed, and the bread was evenly divided among everyone present: the radical redistribution of the world's bread. People ate and drank less during the rest of the conference and a significant amount of money was raised for world hunger programs. But we returned home and our Eucharistic experience was forgotten, for in most parishes Sunday worship had not been reformed.

Some, however, are seeking ways to make sure we will never forget. There is a small Episcopal church in North Carolina in which the children bake the bread and make the wine for the weekly Eucharist. They present it as their offering along with food for the church's food pantry and a bowl of birdseed. After the Eucharist they come forward to break up the remaining bread into the birdseed and at the singing of the final hymn as the hungry birds arrive they put it into a bird feeder outside a window behind the altar. In this same congregation each person is also held accountable for feeding those members of the congregation who are their neighbors. If their neighbor does not attend the liturgy, they take bread and wine from the Eucharist home for them. When they visit them, they read the Sunday's Gospel, pray with them, and share the gifts of God. Perhaps they will learn that we are fed so that we can feed others. Each Advent this same congregation also decorates its halls with balsam. When this season is over, they hold a party and divide up the greens so they can be taken home and put in drawers to smell nice and keep the bugs away. When the balsam is dead, they return it to church and the children make it into incense. Perhaps they will learn that nothing God gives us should be destroyed, for we are the stewards of God's creation.

The church's worship is designed to help us be Christian. We are formed by the liturgy so that we might live a Eucharistic life, a life in gratitude to God. We gather in the grateful awareness that God is with us. We listen and thank God for God's Word. In grateful response to God's Good News we sing a love song of thanksgiving. We pray thankfully, knowing that God is already seeking to do good things for us and all people. In gratitude for the gift of community we share God's peace. In thanksgiving we bring to God what God has already given to us. In thanksgiving we share God's gifts and with gratitude we go forth to bring God's grace to all peoples. Christian stewardship implies a Eucharistic life. When the Eucharist is at the center of our lives then both a proper understanding of stewardship and a faithful life as stewards of God are made possible, indeed are enhanced.

Our weekly participation in the Eucharist is a sign, a symbolic act expressive of our daily life and intended to frame our daily life. The offering within that liturgy is a highly symbolic act, as is every other aspect of the liturgy. The offering makes clear that our lives are to be lives of stewardship. We come to offer what we have done with God's gifts. We offer our talents, our gifts and graces, our money, and our distorted lives, we offer what we have done with God's gifts so that God might use them for God's purposes and we might become cocreators with God, partners in God's ever-present action in history. Thus our humanized universe becomes a divinized one. As a promise that this will occur, we add water to the wine, a symbol of our humanity united with Christ's divinity, signifying the unity of humanity and divinity in Christ and in all of us who live in him. By the mystery of water and wine we share in the divinity of Christ, who humbles himself to share our humanity.

Why we give is as important as what we give. Our money is a symbol of what we have done with our lives. In gratitude we return it to God so that it may become an outward and visible sign of an inward and spiritual grace. The presentation of our monetary gifts is a sacrament of our lives. The body of Christ gathers each week for a ritual act of Eucharist, a sacrament. It then scatters to be a sacrament in the world by living a Eucharistic life. Just as the hour we spend at liturgy each week is to be a sign of how we desire and intend to spend the rest of our time, so the money given is to be a sign of how we desire and intend to spend our financial and material resources during the week.

As we pointed out earlier, the word *liturgy* is descriptive of the lives of Christians. Every human life has two dimensions. One is expressed through cultic life (worship in community) and the other is expressed through daily life (activity in society). Our cultic life is dominated by subjective experience. It is nurtured by the arts, that is, by dance, drama, poetry, music, and the graphic arts. It is best expressed through symbols, myths, and rituals. As such it emphasizes an intuitive way of thinking and knowing. It comes first in time in that it is the natural way of childhood, and it comes first in sequence in that it precedes other ways of thinking and knowing.

Our daily life is dominated by objective reflection and moral action. It is nurtured by the sciences, that is, by theology, a rational activity. It is expressed through signs, concepts, and reflective actions. As such, it emphasizes an intellectual way of thinking and knowing. It comes second in time in that it does not become possible until late childhood or early adolescence, and it comes second in sequence in that it assumes the experiential, intuitive knowledge of which it attempts to make sense and discern a proper response.

Liturgical Catechesis

In regard to liturgy, catechesis plays four roles. First, catechesis provides the community with a means for initiating persons into its ritual life and for reflecting on the meaning of participation for the life of faithful stewardship. Second, catechesis takes place explicitly within the Service of the Word or the Rite of the Catechumens, that part of the liturgy in which we proclaim and respond to the Word. Third, catechesis takes place implicitly throughout the totality of the liturgy insofar as our symbolic actions in the ritual shape our understandings and ways of life. Because this is true, we must take seriously what we know about learning as we plan the Service of the Word and be more intentional about our ritual actions so that they aid in our formation as stewards of God. Fourth, catechesis aids the community to integrate its cultic life and its daily life.

This last is one of the most important, neglected roles of catechesis properly understood: to provide us with an opportunity to reflect on our lives and thereby prepare for true participation in the Eucharist, and to provide us with an opportunity to reflect on our participation in the Eucharist and thereby prepare for more meaningful, purposeful, mindful, and faithful daily life. A faithful congregation that desires to live as stewards of God needs *not only* to reform its educational ministry so that daily life and ritual cultic life are integrated. If I could do whatever I desired, I would bring all ages in a congregation together each week for an hour before the Sunday Eucharistic liturgy to reflect on their lives in the light of the Christian story and together to prepare for their ritual as an expression of their communal life in Christ. Then I would have the community gather after the liturgy to reflect on how they ought to live during the next week and how they might be aided to live in that manner as an outgrowth of their participation in the liturgy. Then and only then will the celebration of the Eucharist make possible living a Eucharistic life, only then will those called by their baptism to be stewards of God live lives of true stewardship. So it is that liturgical catechesis is at the heart of practical theology and at the foundation of faithful stewardship by believers in Jesus Christ and members of his church.

All this may sound idealistic, but I have seen it occur. I once visited a small Episcopal church situated in the middle of a large city. When I arrived about one hundred and fifty persons had gathered. Every age was present. In the front of the nave was a rug and a toy box. A number of small children were quietly playing. The priest sat in the rear. A laywoman was leading the group in discussion. She asked if anyone brought with them any news or concerns. A woman raised her hand to announce that she had just learned she was pregnant. Everyone applauded. The laywoman leading the session asked if she and her husband would like the community to help them prepare for the birth of their baby. They said yes and the priest went off to ask another couple if they would assume that responsibility. An older man raised his hand and said, "Does the church have anything for someone who is hurt?" "What do you mean?" he was asked. "Well," he said, "if you hurt someone you can go to confession and get a new start, but what about the person who is hurt?" The woman answered, "Of course we do, it is the rite of anointing; it's for all hurts, not just physical ones. Would you like that today?" "Yes!" he said. A young woman then announced that she had just gotten a new job as a hotel clerk and she wanted to make her job a ministry. She had written a statement on Christian service and hoped the congregation would offer her its blessing. An older man stood up and explained that everyone knew that he was unhappy with the new prayer book, but that he had just learned that some members of the congregation were cutting their pledges because they were also upset. He said he wanted publicly to tell them that he was increasing his pledge as of this Sunday because he believed the ministry of the community was more important than his preferences.

Next the Gospel lesson was read from the New English Bible. Everyone in the pews followed the Jerusalem Bible translation. They discussed the meaning of the lessons and shared how these lessons touched their lives and illumined them. Persons were chosen to read the lessons and to lead the prayers for the people. The children who had made the bread for communion were chosen to take the offering. Hymns were picked and then, as everyone walked about to greet each other, to introduce newcomers and visitors, the procession began. During the service the couple and their sponsors came forward for a commissioning as well as prayers for the baby in the mother's womb; the rite of anointing was celebrated; so was a commissioning to Christian service. During the offering the children brought forward three bags of food for the church food pantry, as well as the money offering and the bread and wine. Everyone, including babies, communicated.

After the prayer of thanksgiving following communion the woman who had led the preparation for the liturgy came forward, and Coke, coffee, and donuts were passed out. She asked about what they were going to do during the next week. Someone said that they needed volunteers for the church's soup kitchen and a number offered to help. Another person explained that they needed some folks who spoke Spanish to help with an English program. Another said that the money they had collected as loans for people out of work had dwindled and they hoped that if anyone could help, they would do so this week. The group was then asked how they might minister during the week to those who were named as suffering. Some children made a number of suggestions and offered to help. Then the woman leading exclaimed, "Let us go forth to love and serve the Lord." Everyone shouted, "Thanks be to God," and departed as they sang a hymn.

It was a joyous event. Liturgical catechesis for stewardship had been modeled. I wish it could be so in every parish, every Lord's day. It can of course, if only we would will it.

Chapter Five

Life as Seeking After Another's Good: Moral Catechesis

Duke's vice-president for student affairs asked me if I would be on the university's X-rated film review board. I accepted the responsibility as good stewardship of my knowledge, abilities, and time. The experience has not been easy. Recently a number of Duke undergraduates decided to make a test case of the university's negative norms concerning X-rated films. They petitioned to show a Japanese film that won numerous international awards. It related a true historical event, it was an authentic look at sex in Japanese culture, and it was an extremely fine artistic film. It just happened to be about violent sex. Following our viewing most everyone argued that it should be shown. They argued history, culture, artistic quality, and the value of individual freedom of access. I became immediately unpopular when I suggested that there may have been two values in conflict. One was freedom of access, which they had defended—but the other was community responsibility. I pointed out that sex crimes and violence were a serious problem and that we had a responsibility to the community to discourage such acts. I

couldn't get anyone to understand the issue from a communal perspective. From their perspective, it was simply a matter of individual freedom. In my final remarks I suggested a way out of the
value conflict. I proposed that a panel of three scholars—one in Japanese culture, one in Japanese history, and one in film—introduce
the film. I further proposed that a number of staff from Counselling
and Psychological Services lead a small group discussion following
the film so as to deal responsibly with any feeling that might be
aroused. Most of the faculty and students present were unhappy
with this idea, but the vice-president bought it. Since then I've had
the opportunity to reflect on what I said. The more I have done so,
the more I have found myself asking questions related to stewardship.

It is startling to see how little attention is given to stewardship in
general introductions to moral theology and how little attention
writers on stewardship give to moral theology. But a few understand. One theological ethicist who does is Stanley Hauerwas. I
keep returning to his book, *A Community of Character* (published
by University of Notre Dame Press), for insight. His arguments are
particularly helpful because they relate to stewardship. Take, for
example, his discussion of abortion. He argues that Christians are
taught to respect life, not as an end in itself, but as a gift created by
God. Thus life is respected because all life serves God. Respect for
human life is but a form of our respect for all life. The Christian prohibition against taking life rests not on the assumption that human
life has overriding value, but on the conviction that it is not ours to
take. The Christian prohibition against abortion derives not from
any assumption of the inherent value of life, but rather from the
understanding that as God's creatures we have no basis to claim
sovereignty over life. The value of human life, he argues, is God's
value and our commitment to protect it is a form of our worship of
God as a good creator, a trustworthy redeemer, and a sure per-

fecter. The question underlying abortion is not "When does life begin?" but, "Who is life's true sovereign?" The Christian respect for life is first of all a statement not about life but about God.

Hauerwas uses the same form of argument to deal with all moral issues and each finally comes down to the issue of stewardship, namely, who is sovereign, who is the owner, who is the trustee. As he writes, the problem of slavery is not that it violated the inherent dignity of humanity but that as a people for whom Christ is Lord we discover that we cannot worship together at the table of the Lord if one claims an ownership over others that only God has a right to claim. The rights of children, the rights of women, the rights of minorities are all founded on the theological principle of human life as stewardship.

Is it any wonder that we are such poor stewards of human life? Consider: in 1978 about fifty thousand people in the United States died in motor vehicle accidents. About twenty-seven thousand of these people were in the front seat of an automobile at the time of the accident that caused their death. Although lap-shoulder belts were available to the occupants in the majority of these cars, it was estimated that fewer than 5 percent of those fatally injured had taken the trouble to put them on. Estimates of the effectiveness of lap-shoulder belts in reducing the incidence of fatalities range from 40 to 80 percent. During the presidency of Gerald Ford a bill was introduced in Congress that would have required an interlocking lap-shoulder belt and ignition system. Mr. Ford declined to sign the bill into law. The issue seemed clear: Does the government have the authority to protect citizens from themselves? The stated values in conflict were communal responsibility and benfit vs. individual freedom. No one argued about our trusteeship of human life.

The particular stewardship issues we face are complex; there are no simple answers and no single right approach. Without a theological-moral dimension to stewardship it can easily become irrelevant or unfaithful.

The Scriptures contain a vision of society in which the wealth of one person cannot be based upon the exploitation of another and where the conviction that we are all members of a single human family leads those with abundance to supply the wants of all others until the goal of equality is reached (2 Cor. 8:14). The Bible pictures a God who wants us to live as stewards of human life and the natural world. All material resources are to be used to create a world of *shalom*, a world not only of peace, but of well-being, health, harmony, justice, unity, freedom, equity, and community. The central vision in the Bible for life in this world is that of all creation as one, every creature in community with every other, living in harmony and security toward the joy and well-being of every other creature.

The Scriptures do not support the individualism characterized by our culture; rather, they understand human nature as communal. The Scriptures, therefore, also take exception to the popular notion of the absolute right of private property. The earth belongs only to God (not to any person) and therefore cannot be held by anyone perpetually. That is why in the year of the Jubilee (one in every fifty) all land reverts back to its original owner (Leviticus, Chapter 25). In fact, the purpose of the year of Jubilee was to provide for a regular redistribution of wealth so that the poor would never get poorer and the rich richer. Why? Because all wealth was viewed as belonging to God and therefore to all equally. The Scriptures declare war on materialism, which is a preoccupation with material reality that ignores or denies the spiritual; on hedonism, a preoccupation with pleasure or material happiness as the chief goal of life; and on narcissism, a preoccupation with the love of oneself, especially one's physical attributes. For the Scriptures our love is to be directed to God and neighbor, the chief goal of life is doing God's will, and reality is comprised of both a material and spiritual nature.

Most of us have been socialized to live acquisitively. But Jesus proposed a different motivation for life's activities. His words were: "Beware of all covetousness" (Luke 12:5), and "Whoever would be great among you must be your servant" (Mark 10:43). It is not in self-serving, but in losing one's life in the service of another's good that we find our true selves. "Let no one seek his own good, but the good of his neighbor" (1 Cor. 10:24). Both Jesus and Paul speak of concern for the needy and economic sharing.

God is the owner, we are the trustees. The Scriptures forbid a sense of absolute human ownership of anything in creation. In Genesis God creates men and women to tend it, care for it, and share it with each other. The earth and its resources have been given us in trust so that we may use them to sustain the whole human family. God intends us to be trustees of all possessions, property, and productive capital in our keeping by seeking to use them for God's purposes, that is, for the good of all humanity.

Morality is concerned with our human obligations and responsibilities. To be a moral human being is to be accountable and responsible. The God of the Bible is a convenanting God. God is committed to us and expects our commitment in return: "I will be your God and you will be my people." Sin is infidelity to that covenant, that is, our refusal to live up to our part of the bargain, and idolatry is turning the means God gives us to live in community into ends for which we live selfishly and individually.

In the Scriptures, offenses against neighbor are in the final analysis a betrayal of our covenant with God. Our love of God is to manifest itself in love of neighbor. By the same logic, the deepest malice in our offenses against our neighbor is precisely that they imply a rejection of God. When the Prodigal Son finally repents and returns to his ancestral home, he confesses: "Father, I have sinned against God and against you." It is never one or the other. The love of God and neighbor are irrevocably united.

Human community is only possible if each person assumes responsibility for the welfare of every other human being. For this
end God has brought us into covenant and called us to live in gratitude for God's love of us by loving all others. At the center of this
covenantal relationship lies the Decalogue, which reminds us that:
only God is worthy of unreserved faith, unbounded trust and service; we shall not enshrine any notion, ideology, or interest as God
or allow ourselves to be dominated by them; we shall not lay exclu-
sive claim on God's blessing or call upon God to bless our selfish
purposes; we shall make the continual renewal of our spiritual life
of central importance and both act reverently toward the natural
world and regard those who labor with respect; we shall treat the
elderly with honor; we shall not threaten the lives of others by ag-
gressive or irresponsible behavior; we shall not threaten another
person's marriage or family life; we shall not permit another person
to be treated unjustly; we shall not grasp after what belongs to
someone else or seek for ourselves what belongs to all people.

The Beatitudes remind us that those who are holy and whole are
those who depend on God alone; who identify with the poor, the
hungry, the oppressed, and the needy; who are committed to meeting all human need; who act for the liberation and reconciliation of
all humanity; who generously care for every human person; who
acknowledge that everything comes from God; who have a passion
for justice; who desire nothing for themselves, but are willing to pay
any price for the benefit of all.

We are, as Jesus taught, to love God and love our neighbor.

Material Goods

Christian ethics cannot avoid making judgments concerning material goods. While assigning no inherent or intrinsic value to them,
Christian ethics does make normative judgments concerning their

use. We are called to the faithful use of material goods, not a life of detachment from them; it is possessiveness—keeping for oneself more than one needs in the face of another's need—not having possessions, that is judged negatively. The Gospel principle of poverty is not penury, pennilessness, or destitution; it does not deny necessities, only luxuries.

The ethical implication of Christian stewardship is this: we are trustees of God's wealth and we are therefore to act on God's behalf to make sure it is used for God's purposes, that is, according to God's will. Now that is quite different from the usual contentions that we are stewards of our own wealth and act out of a personal commitment to charity. For the Christian everything in this world belongs to God. That explains why in Christian ethics almsgiving has always been treated under the heading of justice rather than mercy. Giving to meet a neighbor's need is in actuality only giving to others what is rightfully theirs.

Each and every person has inalienable equity in God's patrimony. Therefore, our contributions to individuals in need, to community social service agencies, to the church's mission and ministry, to government taxed programs for human need, are simply obligatory acts of stewardship for which we deserve no thanks or reward. Thus we ought never to think that giving or sharing our material goods are acts of mercy for the less fortunate. We are only given the freedom to be responsible or irresponsible stewards of God's wealth. The implications are vast. They include: for what purposes we use our natural resources; how we care for our environment; how we earn and spend our income; what businesses and industries we support; how we care for those in need; how we distribute our material resources; the nature of the social order we maintain; and the quality of human life we encourage. In short, stewardship is concerned with nothing less than our responsibility to God for every aspect of individual and social life within every aspect of our sociopolitical, economic world order. Stewardship is the active recognition of the sovereignty of God over all creation, over all creative and productive processes in which we humans share, and over the uses to which we put each and every resource and means that come into our care and control.

Buildings, for instance, present an opportunity for stewardship. It is a heresy to downplay buildings. Christian faith is incarnational. Our space defines us; it tells us who we are. Goodness, truth, and beauty are all Christian virtues. To negate one is to harm the others. I recall how students were upset when it was announced that an expensive handcrafted processional cross and altar candles were to be bought for the university chapel. They reasoned that the money should be given for good works. I argued that they had fallen into a heresy of rightly affirming goodness but being so concerned for it that they devalued the beauty without which we might lose that vision necessary for inspiring good works (the test is commitment to both). Buildings are held in trust. It is not buildings, but what they are used for, that is important. I think of how the Chapel of the Cross, where I am a priest associate, is open twenty-four hours a day, seven days a week as a place of hospitality for all sorts of individuals and groups. For some it is simply a place to rest or sleep, to get a cup of the free coffee that is always available, to go into the kitchen and cook a meal with the food provided, or in the case of students to sleep or study in silence. The church building is for ministry. It needs to be cared for and preserved so that this ministry might be possible in the future. To give up church buildings or to let them fall into disrepair is to be poor stewards of these gifts. To make our buildings so valuable that we fear using them is also poor stewardship.

The moral issue of stewardship must focus on economics. The issue, of course, is not just money, but how it is acquired and for what purposes it is spent.

Recall when Paul was at Philippi and used by God to bring healing and sanity to a slave girl who had brought her owners great gain
through her soothsaying. The owners seized Paul and Silas and
dragged them before the rulers complaining that they were disturb-
ing the social order. Paul was permitted to preach undisturbed until
he struck at economic issues. It has always been so. Consider the stir
caused in Amarillo, Texas, by the once beloved Roman Catholic
Bishop Leroy Matthiesen, who simply established a Peace Fund to
help workers at a local plant that manufactures nuclear weapons to re-
locate and find new jobs if their present jobs violated their consciences.

The love of money has always been a root of social evil. Recall
that slavery was only abolished in the North because it was not profitable and it was on its way out in the South until the invention of
the cotton gin made it once again profitable. One of the causes of
racial and sexual prejudice is the fear of economic competition.
Smoking may be a health hazard, but for economic reasons the government, while warning people not to smoke, economically supports the growing of tobacco. Unjust wages and labor practices are
also supported on the grounds that if the cost of production is
raised, investors will receive less profit on their investment. Inadequate housing, grudging food distribution programs, declining social welfare and health programs, and deteriorating schools are per-
petuated because people with money are unwilling to be taxed so
that the good of all might be met. Modern war is an evil that threat-
ens the existence of civilization, yet preparation for war is at least
partly motivated by economic exploitation and greed. We continue
to have difficulty addressing issues related to ecology because of the
money involved in correcting them. Economic determinism may
not be an adequate understanding of history, but economics surely
plays a major role in almost every decision we make; human rights
and moral issues appear to take a back seat to "economic realities,"
as they are called.

Every Christian, rich or poor, is responsible for how our economy works, but the rich tend to have more power and influence and so bear a greater responsibility to see that the economy works for the benefit of all. Stewardship surely does not imply the complete renunciation of the ownership of material possessions, but it does imply the acknowledgment that we are held accountable for how these possessions are acquired and how they are used. It also provides us with a general principle to guide our moral decisions, namely, that the good of all people is to be served. The Gospel ethic is clear. Just as God gives us what we need and not what we deserve, we are to do likewise, that is, to seek the good of all others. We are to see that others receive what they need and not what they deserve.

In the past, in a barter economy, it may have been possible to conceive of persons sharing their products and services with those they knew who were in need. But today we live with a money economy on a planet that has become a global village. It is difficult to know who is in need, and it is more difficult to address the needs of those we know about. Everything we do seems to affect someone else, at least indirectly. In a money economy it is difficult to see the results of our giving. It is also difficult to control how it will be used. In a small closely knit community, service to the neighbor may still be personally performed, but this kind of service is no adequate solution to the neighbor's need in today's complex money economy. We simply must give large sums of money to national and international agencies to use on our behalf. We must engage in political action to influence the proper use of our national economy and engage in social action to influence economic life in the public sector so it will serve the social good. Christian stewardship in our modern world necessitates such sociopolitical-economic actions. Moral theology should aid us in our decisions and moral catechesis should equip us to perform faithful, responsible actions.

In traditional moral theology there were four natural virtues. The first was justice. Its purpose was to govern our conduct toward others. Justice was understood as seeking after the good of all others, that is, to establish wholeness, health, harmony, and prosperity for every living person. As such, justice was the negation of self-interest. Temperance and fortitude were the second and third natural virtues. Their purpose was to govern our concern for ourselves. Temperance implied the mastery of self-need, so that we might engage in the right and proper use of creation. Fortitude implied resistance to all those principalities and powers, those trials and temptations that led us away from seeking the good of others. The fourth virtue was prudence. Its purpose was to govern the other three. As such, prudence implied practical wisdom, that is, the habit of referring all concerns to the criteria of God's will. This later natural virtue necessitated three theological virtues: faith, hope, and love. Faith focused on perception or the gift of seeing reality as God sees it so that we might know God's will; hope implied anticipation or the gift of passion to do God's will; and love focused on action or the gift of being able to will the good of the other; thus love was not an erotic activity of mutual need gratification or a filial activity of shared interest, but an agapeic activity of seeking after the other's good, no matter what the cost.

There is no way to act like a Christian apart from being one, that is, apart from participation in the life of a Christian faith community, the church. We need to be reminded that there is no Christian morality, that is, there is no particular action that can claim the name Christian and thereby rule out all other actions as being non-Christian. We carry with us no advanced knowledge of God's will for every concrete situation. But there is a Christian ethic. That is, as Christians we live within a tradition, we bear a story of what God has done, a vision of what God intends, guiding principles and norms for human life, a community to aid our reflection, and a commitment to open ourselves to discern God's will. Nevertheless, it is always in some particular historical situation that we are called upon to reflect and act. We need to be aware that each situation is unique and so calls for an analysis of the facts surrounding it, a knowledge of alternative actions as well as anticipated and actual consequences, an awareness of our motives, and a clear understanding of what is at stake.

A Christian character is the aggregate of qualities (terminal and instrumental values, convictions, dispositions, attitudes, habits, and behavior) resulting from life in a Christian story-formed faith community. It is informed and shaped by a Christian perception of life and our lives, lived in a covenant relationship with God and directed toward the realization of our true humanity through self-giving love for the good of all.

A Christian conscience is the intentional activity of a whole person (thinking, feeling, willing) in conscious loyalty to Jesus Christ and his church, making moral judgment on what is a faithful act (God's will) in the light of the church's teaching and the facts of a particular historical situation. The church's teaching, within whose authority we stand, is founded upon Scripture (the memory of what God has done and vision of what God intends), tradition (the beliefs and ethical norms upon which the church is founded), and reason (the rational striving in community amidst contemporary experience to discern and be obedient to God's will).

Moral catechesis aims not at morality (right conduct) but at maturity. Christian morality is a by-product of Christian maturity; its concern is ultimately with who we are in our relationship with God and each other. Too many Christian educators are solely concerned with shaping conduct or overt behavior; that is not enough for the Christian. For example, the law "you shall not kill" is satisfied if we do not physically harm another person, but if we hate someone with a deep and abiding unforgiving loathing that is restrained only by fear of retaliation, we are from a Christian perspective murderers. Why? Because it is who we are in our relationship with another that judges moral action; who we are is what we are disposed to be, which in this case in its intent is murderous. Moral catechesis is concerned therefore not only with acts performed but persons who do the acting. It is our being as well as our doing that must be the focus of our attention.

Moral Catechesis

Moral catechesis assumes that we need to learn that our identity is in who we are and not in what we have. We need to learn not to use things to protect us from the pain of intimacy with God and vulnerability to neighbor. We need to learn that the material world is a wonderful and awesome gift to be appreciated and used in the service of love and not to be used up, destroyed, or selfishly possessed. We need to learn that we have very few needs, but only wants that can erode our freedom to care for others' needs; we need to learn to possess nothing and no one. We need to learn to accept and affirm our gifts and graces, our talents, and to use them for the benefit of others. We need to learn to accept joy or sadness, prosperity or poverty, adversity or benefit, honor or contempt so long as they result in a virtuous life directed to serving the good of others.

As Christians, we confess belief in the Triune nature of God, who creates, redeems, and perfects. We need to acknowledge that this belief affirms the goodness of procreation and the preservation of all life; affirms that all life is of equal value; affirms that the intention of life is wholeness and health for all.

Our character and conscience as Christians are shaped by the overt and covert influences and experiences of life in an intentional story-formed community that shares a common memory, a common vision, a common authority, common rituals, and a common life together.

One night some twenty-five years ago I was leading a youth group in a large suburban church. Two youths were making popcorn in the kitchen. Their voices got louder and louder. Back and forth they shouted, "I'm going to put salt in the popcorn!" "No you're not going to put salt in the popcorn!" And then a body came crashing through the kitchen door. (He put salt in the popcorn.) As they pursued each other out of the church, the others in anger wanted to know what we were going to do with them. They had been ruining everything since kindergarten. I said, "Let's talk about it." By midnight there were only a few still present. They decided to pay for the broken door and invite these two back to make popcorn again next week. As one put it, "in two bowls." I turned to the sixteen-year-old girl next to me and asked, "Why did you do that?" Her answer amazed me. "Well," she said, "that's the way God treats us, isn't it? We keep messing up but God does more than pay for doors. God died so we will know we are loved anyway. He doesn't give us what we deserve and gives us what we need and I guess tonight I just wanted to show I was grateful."

I also recall the early days of the civil rights movement. At the time I was a religious journalist, the editor of *Colloquy* magazine. People were complaining that we never printed any stories of good news. So I went looking for one. I discovered a small Episcopal church in the Deep South that had integrated. I thought that would make a good news story, so I went to interview the senior warden. "What was your motivation for integration," I asked, "was it a matter of social justice or human dignity?" "No," he answered, "it was just that we became aware that we couldn't be the church, a sign of God's kingdom, if we all couldn't gather at the same table, and black and white eat from a common loaf and drink from a common cup."

Moral catechesis is more than classes in decision making. Perhaps that is why Craig Dykstra's recent book on moral catechesis, *Vision And Character* (published by Paulist Press), is so important. For a number of years Christian educators have uncritically accepted the work of Lawrence Kohlberg, who focused his understanding of moral development and education on making judgments about the rightness and wrongness of particular acts, especially when there were conflicts of interest. Dykstra's radical alternative focuses on the way one sees reality and responds to it in the light of that vision. He rightly points out that how people perceive life and their lives determines what they are about and how they live. The stories that we affirm as explaining our lives, the visions or images we hold as the proper ends for life, and the guidelines or virtues our community holds as dear when making decisions—all of these are the keys to moral catechesis. That is why, he explains, you can't separate worship and prayer from moral catechesis, or service that persons participate in together, or life in community. We also forget that the best moral catechesis for children focuses on the foundational concern of shaping character and providing the conscience with the values and ethical norms out of which moral decisions are made. In this regard it is my contention that liturgy, properly understood and celebrated, is the best means for moral catechesis in the childhood years. Of course, in many parishes this will imply a rethinking and reforming of the Sunday liturgy so children can meaningfully participate.

Moral catechesis also necessitates the continual evaluation and mindful designing of faithful communal life. As such, it includes a concern for our social organization, the roles and status of persons in the community as well as the composition of our community; it includes our use of time and space, our language, the nature of human interaction, our orientation to the culture, the role models present as well as the behavior encouraged and supported; it also includes the decision-making processes employed by the community in its daily life.

There are a host of persons asking moral questions related to stewardship. I wonder sometimes, however, if our classes on moral issues at church help much. We all face the dilemma of discussing theoretical issues in church and then having to make practical decisions where we live and work. I have always thought that the church would be wiser if it brought people together where they live and work to reflect on their lives. I know parishes that have done that. I know of a group of physicians who meet in the doctors' dining room of the hospital for an hour once a week. Someone presents a troubling case and then they try to relate their faith to a possible solution. I know of a church that once leased a car from a railroad. Their parishioners bought tickets from them and they turned their two-hour commute into a context for moral catechesis. After reading the *New York Times* and the *Wall Street Journal* with coffee they turned to case studies written by their fellow commuters. I know of a group of parents who gathered each week in someone's home for dessert to discuss issues related to bearing and raising children. I know a group of farmers who gathered once a week for breakfast before picking up supplies to discuss issues of Christian faith and agriculture. And I know of a group of laborers who gathered over lunch to discuss labor problems as they related to their faith. The list could go on, but they each followed a procedure that has been advocated by Thomas Groome in his significant work *Christian Religious Education* (published by Harper & Row). In that book he recommends and describes "shared praxis." It has five movements or steps. First, persons are invited to name their own present activity concerning the issue before them. Second, they are invited to reflect on why they do what they do and what the likely or intended consequences are of their actions. Third, they share in discovering the Christian story concerning the issue at hand and the faith response it invites. Fourth, they are invited to appropriate the Christian story to their lives in a dialectic with their own stories. And fifth, they are given the opportunity to choose a personal faith response for the future that they believe is faithful to the Christian vision for life.

Learning this process of rational reflection when joined with experience and action in a community of Christian faith provides the necessary components for moral catechesis. The key, however, remains in our being able to form a community whose memory, vision, rituals, and common life together express and exemplify a Christian view of stewardship.

Chapter Six

Life as Relationship: Spiritual Catechesis

It was ludicrous. The course title was "Pastor as Spiritual Guide." It met each Monday evening for three hours. The structure was simple. We began with an informal Eucharist that included meditation on Scripture. Each week a book on spirituality was to have been read and we discussed our spiritual journeys as they were illumined by the readings. Then we participated in a spiritual exercise, which was followed by reflection in the form of a lecture and discussion. We closed the evening with fifteen minutes of silence and compline. We were three weeks into the course. Four students made an appointment to see me. When they arrived they told me how disappointed they were with the course; one was angry. They had numerous complaints, like why did we have to worship each week, but they were most upset about the fifteen minutes of silence. One said that they were paying to learn about spirituality and they expected more in the form of lectures. Another commented that he didn't find the time of silence very useful, especially in the light of the fact that they had so much to learn and that this was the only course in spirituality they intended to fit into their course of study. Two others simply said it was a waste of time. I thought an intellectual response best, so I told them about Saint Benedict's way, formulated in the fifth century, which included work, study, and praise. I pointed to the New Testament invitation to do everything in the Name of Jesus (Col. 3:17), study the Scriptures (2 Pet. 1:19), and praise God in psalmody (Eph. 5:19), and told them of Saint Bendict's important contribution to spirituality, which was bringing them together as a unit, each aspect to be emphasized equally. I explained how he thought the best training for ministry included *opus manuum* (manual work, which in our case was readings and discussions), *lectio divina* (spiritual reading, which in our case was praying the Scriptures), and *opus Dei* (divine work or worship, which in our case was Eucharist, compline, and silence). Of these three, I suggested, the most neglected and difficult for North American students was silence. I shared with them my experience in Japan, where no one would interrupt someone who was in silence doing nothing, for example daydreaming, but they would freely interrupt someone who was busily working. In the United States it is just the opposite, I explained. Time spent in silence, daydreaming, is considered unimportant and unproductive. I recommended that they read Henri Nouwen's small book *The Way of the Heart* (published by The Seabury Press) because it has an important chapter on silence. I gathered that they were not fully satisfied, but they left.

The same day another student in the class came to see me. He wanted to explain that he was working in a church on weekends and so could not attend the retreat we had scheduled. I thought the issue was authority, so I explained that I would be happy to write a note or make a call to explain his absence. He told me I didn't understand. They needed him. He presented a long list of his responsibilities and how important each was to the church's life. I tried to explain that perhaps the people needed him to tell them that he had to go and pray. I pointed out that he could pray for them and that this act might make a greater contribution than his presence. He said I didn't understand and dropped the course.

The stewardship of time and the human need to nurture our relationship with God are essential to faithful trusteeship. Why does it appear so difficult for seminarians to understand? When my advisees come to see me for the first time, I ask them to tell me how their friendship with God is going. Typically they are speechless, which usually means they do not understand the question. I probe further by asking: "What is the quality of the time you spend alone with God each day? What sort of time do you waste with each other? How well do you express intimacy? How well are you able to share feelings honestly? What common experiences have you shared? What have you heard God saying lately?" Their typical response is, "I read the Bible and pray every day, but I don't do any of those things." "That's all right," I respond, "it just means we are only at the beginning of building a relationship." "Have you ever thought," I continue, "that if you treated people the way you treat God, they wouldn't say anything either? Find some time to be alone and silent with God each day," I counsel, "it's essential to your stewardship of time." In our contemporary culture it often seems that time, not money, enslaves us. We typically say, "I do not have time." Just thinking about all we have to do exhausts us. Time has us; we do not have time. We have become the victims of our clocks and calendars. We are so busy we have no time to live in relationship with God. The contemplative life provides us with the redemption of time. Through it we begin to see God in our lives. We awaken ourselves to God in us, we invite God in to every aspect of our lives and we are able to see God in our world around us.

Aquinas wrote: "Prayer is the peculiar proof of religion." Faith, in Luther's judgment, was "prayer, nothing but prayer." Baron von Hügel concluded that "prayer is the essential element of all life." Schleiermacher observed: "To be religious and to pray are really the same thing." Friedrich Heiler declared that "prayer is the heart and center of all religion." In fact, what most distinguishes a religious institution from other voluntary, ideological, or service institutions is its claim to prayer.

Still the word *prayer* lacks clarity. Some think of prayer as distressed cries to the heavens, others a formality before meals and meetings or an experience on mountaintops. Prayer for some is a spontaneous emotional discharge and for others a fixed rational formula to be recited. *Prayer*, as I am using the word, is a generic term to describe every aspect of our conscious relationship with God. Prayer is the method of the spiritual life—daily existence lived in relationship with God, the daily activity of living in the presence of God through adoration, confession, praise, thanksgiving, and petition/intercession.

The spiritual life, then, is a historical life lived with a conscious awareness of God's presence; it is life so lived that our minds, hearts, and wills are united with God's in common historical reflective action. Surely this understanding rules our prayer, in which the world or the self is depreciated or denied, in which the human personality is dissolved or absorbed into a unity with an otherworldly reality. Prayer is not a negative process moving us out of our normal state or condition, a passive resigned contemplation of otherness, nor a striving after emotional ecstasy through the extinction of thought or volition. Prayer is ultimately an ethical activity. History is the peculiar providence of God's revelation and fellowship. Blessedness of life with God is life in this world; in our daily lives we meet and have communion with God.

The Christian life focuses upon the spirit of God in us and in the world; its quest is for an active unity with the God of history. The climax of the Christian life is not enlightenment but unification with the will and activity of God. Christian prayer assumes both a historical awareness and the integration of the receptive and active modes of consciousness.

If prayer is no longer satisfying or if God seems no longer real, it may be because we have turned prayer into speaking formally to God. Only prayerfulness, a radical love of God and neighbor, is fully satisfying. Listening to God and serving with God is true prayer. Prayer implies an engagement with the world, a wrestling with the principalities and powers. Prayer is never an escape from the world or its trials and tribulations. Prayer is a way of life, a relationship with the God who acts in history, lived day by day.

Prayer is not so much telling God as it is listening and responding to God, to God's will, to God's actions. It is not found in attempts to manipulate God or change God's will; it is rather listening and answering God's call to newness of life and action with God in the world. Steve Seger, a rabbi with whom I teach, in response to the question, How do Jews understand prayer? said "During the dry season we never pray for rain, but during the rainy season we always pray for rain." In the Scriptures, prayer is primarily a thanking and recalling of God's presence in one's life and in history, not primarily asking God for something. God is seeking to have us live in and for God's coming community. Prayer is our getting our lives right with God. It ought not to be an exceptional experience.

Paul writes to the Roman community: "I appeal to you . . . by the mercies of God to present [offer] your bodies [whole selves] as a living sacrifice, holy [dedicated] and acceptable to God which is your spiritual worship. Do not be conformed to this world, but be transformed by the renewal of your mind that you may prove what is the will of God, what is good and acceptable and perfect" (Rom. 12:1–2).

This implies behaving in such a way that God's will determines all our behavior, something which only can be achieved if our minds accept as normative God's standards rather than those characteristic of our culture and the times in which we live.

The spiritual life, of course, is not an evasion of intellectual responsibility. We must acquire that disciplined passion for reason and right thinking which is *paideia*. It means literally "bringing up children," which implies the disciplined education of the mind in both its intellectual and intuitive modes. This is obviously not to defend a sterile or passionless intellectualism, but an affirmation of the unity of heart and head, the affective and cognitive domains of human thought.

The process of spiritual growth is the development of consciousness and the wholeness of human life in moral community. As the late Urban Holmes put it, "The outcome of the experience of God in Christ should be a heightened consciousness which becomes the basis for action which is virtuous."[13] Catechesis must support that understanding. Still, a few questions about the processes that lead to that spiritual end are necessary.

The Christian faith is full of enough poignant, provocative specifics to be spoken about directly and bluntly. We need not moralize or theologize about the cross. Talking about the specifics of that death and of that suffering is enough. Let us formulate our own ideas about its meaning in our own lives.

Jesus counsels, "You must love the Lord your God with *all your heart*, with *all your soul* and with *all your mind*. This is the greatest and the first commandment. The second resembles it: you must love your neighbor as yourself. On these two commandments hang the whole law and the prophets" (Matt. 22:37–40). One of the strange things about us modern Christians is the way we treat this teaching of Jesus. We worry far more about people's belief in God than about their love relationship with God. Religious surveys usually try to estimate the number of believers, but rarely do they seek to ascertain if people know God, that is, live in an intimate love relationship with God. One of my students once asked, "Why does the mystical experience, the direct experience of God, seem to fill religious history, but remain absent for most people in our time?"

As we discussed the question, I discovered that most of my students doubted that God was intimately related to their lives or to modern history. Is it any wonder, I thought, that a healthy understanding of our lives as trustees of God's love had eluded us?

The difficulty appears to be in the way we were brought up, even in the church, to believe that all reality can be explained in material terms, understood rationally, and explained on the basis of natural order. The sad thing is that even our science is out of date. We simply have missed the writings of physicists such as Heisenberg, mathematicians such as Gödel, psychologists such as Jung, and biologists such as Eiseley.

Loren Eiseley, the great evolutionary biologist and anthropologist, explains in *The Unexpected Universe* (published by Harcourt Brace Jovanovich) that science since the thirteenth century has clung to the dictum of William of Ockham that the world is always simple, not complicated, and its secrets are accessible to the intellect. Ironically, he continues, in this time of our greatest intellectual and technological triumphs we are forced to admit that William of Ockham's long-honored precepts are merely a projection of our human desire to control and manipulate the world for our own selfish benefit.

In the same book, he tells of the day in which he caught the toe of his shoe in a drain and fell to the sidewalk. Blood from a gash on his forehead cascaded over his face. He found himself murmuring in compassion "Oh, I'm sorry, I'm sorry!" and realized that he was addressing his blood cells as they sacrificed their lives to repair the rent fabric of his being. Through his folly they were suffering and dying like beached fish on a hot pavement for him. For the first time, he loved them consciously. For years he had secretly wanted a miracle and now one had occurred. Eiseley the great scientist has retained a prescientific sense of wonder and awe and so he has discovered that there is more to life than he had imagined.

In 1970 a group of youths from around the world made a pilgrimage to the monastic community at Taizé. When they arrived they explained what they were searching for. A young American woman summed up the convictions of many when she explained that she was searching for a new spiritual depth in her life. Life—at least as she had lived it up until then—had robbed her of an experience of the simple yet mysterious qualities of reality. "My world," she said, "has left me believing that I am a privatized, independent, selfish, pleasure-seeking being. As a result, my life has lost meaning and purpose. Life has become a daily grind of work, eating, and sleeping and I have little commitment to anything other than finding ways of escape from this awful rat race aimed solely at the acquisition of material goods."

Christian faith, of course, affirms the goodness of material goods, but it also asserts their limitations. The material world is good, but it is a limited good, limited in the sense that we cannot make a life out of it. The material world is not an evil to be avoided, but neither is it a good to be possessed or accumulated.

A Spiritual Life

H.A. Williams in his inspiring book *True Christianity* (published by Templegate) helped me to understand that all Christians are called to a life of poverty, chastity, and obedience. Regrettably, these ways of living have been typically understood in literal, negative terms and restricted to those who choose to live in religious community. Properly understood, they provide spiritual foundations for the life of stewardship.

Malnutrition, homelessness, nakedness are destructive of human selfhood and Christians are called to feed the hungry, clothe the naked, and house the homeless. The way of poverty is not to live at subsistence nor is it intended to avoid all of this world's goods. Indeed, poverty understood in negative terms is as much a cause of sin as is affluence. The true way of poverty, however, makes it possible for us not be anxious about acquiring or losing; it helps us to understand that we are more than what we possess; it makes it possible for us to live joyfully in the present; it provides us with the freedom to share; it provides us with the understanding that who we are is more important than what we have. The way of poverty is an attitude of the heart and mind that makes it possible for us to be stewards of God's creation.

Chastity is also a laudatory way of life. Regrettably, chastity has been reduced solely to a negative rule concerning overt sexual behavior. We forget that the way of chastity is an intellectual and emotional way as well as a physical one. Intellectual chastity aims to free us from convention, ideological propaganda, and illusion; it encourages us to seek the power to perceive, discriminate, and discern the Way, the Truth, and the Life. Emotional chastity aims to free us from the superficial, the sentimental, and the artificial; it encourages us to seek the mysterious. Physical chastity, properly understood, aims to free us from lust, pornographic life, and infidelity; it encourages us to seek communion with all persons and with God at the deepest level of our being.

Like poverty and chastity, obedience has acquired a bad name. We all know how it has been corrupted and used by those who desire power to exploit the weak. At its best, however, the way of obedience points to our discovering who we really are or, better, what it is possible for us to be, and how we can be loyal to that insight. Through the virtue of obedience we become fully who we already are. Our baptism tells us what it means to be fully human and humane. To be obedient is to strive to actualize that truth as of our reform and to live into our baptism, to become who we are, children in the family of God. Obedience is not submission to an external authority, indeed, it frees us from that oppression so that we might be loyal to our true selves and enable others to do likewise.

So it is that the way of poverty, chastity, and obedience makes it possible for us to fulfill our calling as stewards of God.

Sin is the denial of our true being . We are stewards of God and we are capable of being God's stewards, but we are inclined (not destined) to live otherwise. Unless we can acknowledge the truth that we are liberated from those principalities and powers that entice us to deny our true being, that we have the potential to actualize our true being, and that we have the possibility to reach perfection or sanctification, the calling to be stewards of God will not be realized.

Pride, Envy, Anger, Sloth, Avarice, Gluttony, and Lust are called the seven deadly sins. Actually they are disordered affections that lead us to sin. If we truly understand this, it will help us to be better stewards of God.

All seven are demonstrations of love gone wrong, of relationships distorted. Each springs from the impulse to love wrongly. They are examples of that perverted, defective, and excessive love that destroys God's intentions for relationship.

Pride. Self-esteem is a proper and healthy affection, but pride results in a narcissism that places self-love above love for others. We cannot properly bear our trusteeship of God's grace, which is intended to be shared with all humanity, when we turn our love in on ourselves.

Envy. Today we live with the widespread assumption that everyone should be able to do, experience, and enjoy everything that anyone else can do. We cease being grateful for or happy in what we are or in what we have because we are concerned about what others have and our desire to have the same. Obviously this works against stewardship, which is life lived in gratitude to God for our gifts and graces.

Anger. Perhaps wrath would be the better word, for the anger this sin describes is "nursed anger," that is, anger that intends or leads to violence. We are a nation of angry people: angry with ourselves, our lot, the world, and life in general. We cannot see the grace in our lives and so we strike out at the world in a spirit of revenge.

Sloth. Sloth is more than idleness; it is the despair resulting from believing we cannot make any difference in the world. It is not giving a damn. One simply cannot be a steward if one doesn't care or get involved.

Avarice. Avarice is not so much the love of possessions as the love of possessing. To buy what we do not need and to become possessed by the temporal objects we have accumulated is indeed the opposite of stewardship.

Gluttony. When the gratification of our appetites takes over our lives and we become addicted, we are gluttonous. When we live with a disrespect for creation and lose our sense of gratitude for that which nourishes our bodies, when we become obsessive about that which does not truly nourish us, we are gluttonous. Greed for bodily comforts makes us less than stewards of God's gifts.

Lust. Lust is not being interested in persons, but only in gratifying our own cravings. Lust is not a sin of the body but against it, it denies that we are part of creation and need to be related to each other and involved with each other. It empties our capacity for loyalty or enduring relationships and eventually makes it impossible for us to love truly.

Spiritual catechesis assumes that proper human affections are those resulting from self-esteem, self-affirmation, self-expression, self-giving, self-sharing, self-enjoyment, and self-actualization, but these healthy affections can be disordered by pride (self-centeredness)—envy (the quest after what is not rightly ours)—anger (desiring to hurt another)—sloth (not caring)—avarice (the love of possessing)—gluttony (addiction to gratifying our appetites)—and lust (using others for our enjoyment). To avoid these disordered affections we need to learn and practice the virtues of humility (acknowledging that all we have and are is a gift from God)—liberality (a concern for others' needs)—meekness (openness to others)—zeal (passionate caring)—generosity (giving away)—temperance (moderation in all things)—and charity (actively seeking the good of others).

Alan Jones of General Theological Seminary introduced me to Graham Greene's novel *Dr. Fisher of Geneva or the Bomb Party* (published by Avon). In it Greene outlines the requirements necessary for human beings to have souls. The first is the willingness to suffer for another. The second is a commitment to a life that is marked by moments of listening and waiting on God. The third is a willingness to pay attention to the deep restlessness of the spirit; that is, becoming aware of the longings, disappointments, brokenness, and incompleteness in our lives. Jones adds a fourth, namely, life in a community that sees Christ in us. Without spiritual companions who see the image of God in us, we are apt to miss it and so lose our souls.

To have a soul is to open ourselves to the world and its needs, to turn acquisitive self-love into self-giving love for others. True solitude transforms us, for in solitude the old self dies and a new self is born. By making ourselves available to God, we find ourselves and God. To pay attention to the deep restlessness in our hearts is difficult in our day, but when we can embrace solitude and silence—when we discover that life is a gift to be shared, not a possession to be defended—we become aware that our worth is not the same as our usefulness. It brings us into community.

President Carter once said, "We have discovered that owning things and consuming things does not satisfy our longing for meaning. We have learned that piling up material goods cannot fill the emotions of lives which have no confidence or purpose."

But contemporary culture is plagued by the passion to possess. The supreme goal of our culture is to have and to have more and more. We live in a society that rests on private property, profit, and power. To acquire and to own are the sacred and inalienable rights of the individual in our society. The noun, a proper denotation for a thing, has slowly begun to dominate the verb in our common speech. Having has replaced being, wrote Erich Fromm.[14] We have a degree, a job, a home. We even have friends. To consume is one form of having and perhaps the most dangerous. In an affluent industrial society we are what we have and what we consume.

Having refers to things and passivity, being refers to experience and activity. To be human is to be active. To be active means to give expression to one's faculties, talents, and the gifts with which we are endowed. It means to discover and renew oneself, to grow and to share. Thereby, our contemplative life and daily life are integrated.

One of the most serious issues people have to face today is the realization that they are lovable and loved. Without that assurance, it is difficult to love others, to give of ourself or our possessions to another. If we do not feel loved, we turn our love in on ourselves. When we do not feel lovable we acquire things and possessions in order to feel better about ourselves. Those who engage in spiritual direction know the severity of this problem. The first aim of spiritual life is to discover that we are indeed loved and lovable, and thereby free to live as God's ambassadors of grace. Because we are loved, we can love. Because God gives, we are enabled to give. Accepting God's great generosity sets us free to model that generosity toward others.

Inner simplicity results in an outward simplicity of life-style. Unless we experience the inward reality of letting go of our need to control, we cannot be freed to live simply or make our lives and resources available to others. Because we lack the inner peace of a divine center, our need for security has led us to an insane attachment to things. Our lust for affluence is psychotic. We crave for what we do not need, we buy what we do not want.

Richard Foster in his book *The Celebration Of Discipline*[15] lists ten controlling principles for the life of simplicity. To paraphrase: First, we should buy things for their usefulness and not for their status, that is, buy only what is essential rather than what is desirable. Second, reject anything that is becoming addictive whether it be coffee, cigarettes, television, or computer games. Third, develop the habit of giving things away, especially if we are becoming attached to them or if they are not being used regularly. Fourth, free ourselves from gadgets that use energy and return to using hand power. Fifth, learn to enjoy things without owning them and make everything we own public by sharing it. Sixth, develop a deeper appreciation of creation. Seventh, buy only what we need and what we can afford. Eighth, make honesty and integrity the distinguishing characteristics of our speech and life. Ninth, reject anything that will breed the oppression of others and do not buy from those who do not treat their labor justly. And tenth, shun anything that would distract us from our main goal of being—to seek first God's kingdom and righteousness.

The faithful and wise steward will always be possessed with a great longing to know and do the will of God. That explains why one of the greatest responsibilities of stewardship is prayer, praying "may your kingdom come and your will be done."

Spiritual Catechesis

In Dostoevski's *Brothers Karamazov*, the saintly Russian monk tells us that " . . . prayer is an education." Prayer teaches us how to live as stewards of God. To pray as Jesus prayed is to offer our lives back to God, the God who gave them to us. Without constant attention to prayer, we will be socialized and drawn into an understanding of life and our lives that will make the life of stewardship difficult. There is almost nothing in our culture to support a healthy understanding of life as trusteeship. Only with a major attention to prayer can life be lived faithfully.

We also need to learn to pray, to think and live always in the presence of God. This is not easy, since even though we want to be with God, to love and worship God, there are parts of our lives we want to withhold. To learn to pray is to be disciplined. We need to set aside special times and places each day to do nothing else but work at developing a friendship with God. If all life is to be lived gratefully, we need to establish certain times and places to express thanksgiving.

The disciples asked Jesus "Teach us to pray" and he did, through his words and his example. He taught them that true prayer is opening ourselves to God and when God reveals what it is God desires for us to be and do, to ask for it, knowing that in the moment we do our prayer will be answered. In the "Our Father" Jesus revealed the questions God wants us to ask each day so that we might be faithful. Jesus said to ask: What do you want to make possible in my life this day that neither I nor any other human being can make possible? What do you want to make holy and whole in my life this day? How can your kingdom come through me this day? What are my Gethsemanes about which I need to say your will be done? What nourishment do I need for the day? For what do I need to be forgiven and whom do I need to forgive? From what do I need to be protected? To be stewards of God is to open ourselves to God's power in our lives so that it can be channeled through us to others.

One of the truths emphasized by Thomas Merton in his writings is that human beings have a fundamental duty to orientate their entire being and lives toward God. For Merton our spiritual life is not primarily our work; rather it is the work of God in us.[16] Hence, one's life of stewardship is related directly to the experience of union with God. Because we are called to this relationship with God we find our true identity in God alone. To be human we must become conscious of the fact that the only way to live is to live in a world that is charged with the presence and activity of God. Above all, he explains, it is spirituality that underscores the intimate relationship that should exist between humans and God.

The spiritual life necessitates our becoming keenly aware of the presence and goodness of God in our lives; we must enter into an intimate relationship with God since the fulfillment of our destiny can only be found in this relationship. Only if we experience the transformation of consciousness that results from a union with a living and personal God can the life of stewardship be actualized.

Prayer is the arena within which God and humans communicate themselves to each other and live in a conscious union. This life of prayer has a number of qualities essential to our lives as stewards of God's gifts. The first quality is gratitude. Thanksgiving is at the heart of our relationship with God. Secondly, prayer assumes an attitude of awe, wonder, and dependence. Third, prayer assumes a willingness to listen and discern the will of God. Fourth, prayer assumes a desire to accept and request what God desires. And fifth, prayer assumes discipline. Relationships must be carefully and consciously nurtured or they die. Our union with God is a gift God genuinely wishes to bestow on us. And God asks of us above all only the generosity to cooperate in being faithful trustees of God's unmerited gifts. God blesses and fills the lives of those who do with the life that results from accepting death, the peace that is beyond human understanding, and the joy that comes when we embrace suffering.

How we perceive the world and our lives determines how we experience reality and how we live day by day. No aspect of human consciousness, therefore, is more important than the imagination. Regrettably, in our culture the imagination is often destroyed by education. Few things are more vital for children than the enhancement and enlivening of their imagination. Through dance, music, drama, poetry, and the graphic arts children can be introduced to the story and vision that underlies Christian faith. Indeed, one might argue that such activities are at the heart of quality ascetical catechesis for the young. Later when youths and adults turn to disciplined meditation this imagination can be nurtured and used.

The imagination is foundational to the *Spiritual Exercises* of Ignatius Loyola. Individuals are taught here to hold an image up before their consciousness—the image of Christ, the resurrection, the Virgin Mary. By so doing, they then become open to the spiritual reality that these images picture and symbolize. As a result, our imaginal sense and affection are awakened. Through this process persons not only come into contact with spiritual reality itself, but know it in a new way. By living the Christian story and vision imaginatively, we can be brought into actual contact with them in our own day. In the Greek Orthodox tradition, imaginative prayer is reinforced by the use of icons. As objects of devotion, these religious paintings become a window into eternity. Through the use of the imagination they reveal and establish relationships with the spiritual dimensions of reality, they become sacraments, outward and visible signs of an inward and spiritual reality.

We should make better use of the close-at-hand in our teaching. The simplest things can help us formulate the ideas of God as Creator and Provider. We Christians overtalk creation. We advance theories, historical and theological, about creation—losing not only wonder, mystery, and awe, but also meaning. Let us use the most ordinary things in talking about beginning, growth, and change: rocks and water, trees and clouds.

We need to watch the leaves fall into the brook and talk about this imaginatively and at length, and perhaps after some time a great meaning will come through: Nothing lasts forever. A stream once flowing will be clogged and perhaps made stagnant by falling leaves.

We ought not to be afraid of repetition, knowing that there is yet more to be grasped. Far better, we would think, to say over and over again to a questioning person, "Christ is risen. Christ is risen," than to give an elaborate and oftentimes confusing explanation of the resurrection.

We need to use the sudden and the unexpected in our teaching. Again, we are bothered by the discourse, argument, and presentation in Christian education. We believe that the mind can be opened only through an experience that is brisk and startling. Encountering the unexpected through the questioning of a teacher or the discovery of something new in an experience is like seeing a door opening. We must be ready to provide that unexpected question, observation, or perhaps silence that will allow the door to click open or the clock to strike.

We must also consider the body. We Christians are so intellectual. Life is emotional and physical. It would seem important in our worship, for example, to get up and move to a special place, as some do, to receive the bread and wine. We are not rigid about the position of the body, or sitting in meditation, but we do say that this important discipline requires some different and definite posture of the body. If the movement of the hands or the body is involved with emotional participation, it becomes educational.

Perhaps most crucial, we must acknowledge that learning is a process that goes from the inside to the outside. Too often we try to push things into people, and our pushings are brushed aside. Learning is like the process of a chick hatching from an egg; the chick hatches by pecking from within. A blow from the outside will destroy the hatching process. Many of our programs have little to do with the genuine questions people are asking on the inside. Classes on doctrine and perfunctory study groups are all too often unconnected to the genuine questions and needs of people.

If we stress the incarnation of God's presence, we must believe that God is somehow at work in this educational motion from the inside to the outside. We need to encourage people to trust their questions, to be open about them, and to follow their own maturation or hatching process.

Urban T. Holmes was among the most intellectually stimulating and creative minds in the field of spiritual theology. In *A History of Christian Spirituality* (published by The Seabury Press), he developed a descriptive analysis for a psychology of prayer that I have adopted for the purpose of understanding the various ways by which persons can be nurtured as Christians. My contention is that a broad understanding of Christian nurture integrates four modes of spiritual life. First is an intellectual, speculative, sensate mode consisting of meditation on Scripture and leading to insight, whose heresy is rationalism with its tendency toward dogmatism and an excessive concern for reason and right thinking. Second is a volitional, speculative, nonsensate mode consisting of moral actions and active prayer leading to witness, whose heresy is moralism in judging culture and excessive concern for right actions. Third is an affective, emotive, sensate mode consisting of pious devotions and affective prayer leading to presence, whose heresy is pietism with its tendency toward anti-intellectualism and excessive concern for feelings and right experiences. And fourth is an intuitive, affective nonsensate mode consisting of emptying and contemplative prayer leading to mystical union, whose heresy is quietism with its tendency toward neglect of the social world and an excessive concern for absorption into God.

Each of us, due to our unique personality, being a combination of heredity and culture, is more at home in one of these modes. Various schools of spirituality focus on one of the modes, at least for a point of entry. All should affirm the truth and value of the others. Each seeks balance and integration and works to counter the heresy of others. Christian nurture needs to acknowledge these differences and aid persons both to fully develop what is most natural for them and to expand their spiritual life to include the others.

The course we are traveling (often called curriculum) has multiple understandings. For some it is understood as an assembly line where persons are molded. Teachers (adults) are skilled technicians, students (children and youths) are valuable pieces of raw material. The process is one of helping each individual seed to reach its predetermined potential.

Both understandings, when translated into educational designs, seem to require the formulation of objectives, strategies to reach them, and a means for evaluating success. Dorothee Soelle, the theologian, comments in her book on religious experience, *Death By Bread Alone* (published by Fortress Press), that in a time when learning theories tend more and more to be reduced to a technical model informed by physics or biology, displaying the framework of the conditions under which we learn and experience—conditions that are then researched and put into operation—the idea of journey becomes a necessary countermodel. I agree. Our spiritual journeys have proven to us that the experiences most important in life cannot be derived through a process of input-output. I contend, therefore, that a wiser understanding for Christian nurture and the spiritual life is a pilgrimage comprised of pilgrims of all ages sharing a journey toward wholeness and holiness; aware that there is more to life than meets the eye, we search together to find our true lives.

Henri Nouwen once commented that Christian nurture necessitates three things: first, someone who is searching; second, someone who is willing to make her or his life a resource for another; and third, the conviction that if there is to be any knowledge, it will come from a source beyond both. This has been my experience also. Curiosity is a human quality. Children are born curious and remain so until they are taught otherwise. Too often, in the name of education, we discourage searching. All too typically in churches, children are encouraged to be passive and receptive to our efforts to give them information about truth. Too frequently we focus our teaching efforts on skills or techniques and neglect sharing our lives. We tend to search for educational methods rather than the more difficult and somewhat threatening responsibilities of revealing our innermost strivings to find the meaning of our own lives. Too often we are tempted to do things to or for children believing that we have the truth they need. I am more convinced than ever that Christian nurture necessitates persons of all ages sharing with each other their strivings, which can offer the Way and the Truth and the Life. The spiritual life we all quest for comes, however, as a gift to those who share life together in a community of faith.

To help others on their pilgrimage we need to be compassionate. We need to avoid the temptation to laugh at others' ignorance or limitations, to correct others' errors, or to do everything to or for others. We rather need to be able to share, to live with others, to be gentle and patient. We do not need to have all the answers, nor need we feel we have arrived. We only need to be able to say, "I have no solutions, but I will not leave you alone in your search." Prepared only by our own discipline of prayer and meditation, we need only ask, "Where do you want to go—would you like me to go with you?" Or, "I am going home—would you like to join me?" In either case, we say, of course, that all of us will have to find our own way. The best guide on a spiritual journey is one who does not need to be helpful or needed, one who does not try to bear the responsibility for another life, but who can leave others in the hands of God—and get a good night's sleep. To be a guide is to avoid expectations or imposition of personal causes; to avoid giving answers, information, advice, solutions, and help. The process involves a willingness to wait and to encourage persons to get in touch with their own struggles, pains, doubts, questions, and ambiguities.

It is a humble responsibility that cannot be learned the way one can learn skills for teaching. It is a responsibility based on the wisdom that the best way to explain a spiritual dimension is to make it possible for someone else to find the same meaning. All one can do is take responsibility for one's own spiritual growth and be willing to be with others as they do likewise. We teach others to be spiritual and pray by living with them a life of prayer.

Therefore, we need to be warned against the temptation to teach technique. Learning in the spiritual life is an art and not a science. Worse, idolatry is turning spiritual means into ends.

Perhaps the best example I know of a Christian community providing the sort of spiritual catechesis I believe necessary for stewardship is the Church of the Savior in Washington, D.C. There are others, of course, the Sojourner Community, the Church of the Redeemer, Koinonia Partners, the Fellowship of Hope, to name just a few. Each was founded by persons who were willing to let go of forms and structures that seemed safe and permanent. Still, the same is possible for any congregation that is willing to journey inward and open itself to the leading of God's spirit.

Elizabeth O'Connor has movingly described the Church of the Savior in her books, *Call to Commitment, Journey Inward, Journey Outward,* and *The New Community* (all published by Harper & Row). She once pointed out that the vows we make when we become members of the church of Jesus Christ are more than an oath to stick around with a particular group of people, they are a commitment to a total inner transformation. For the only thing that matters, wrote Saint Paul, is a new creation (Gal. 6:15). In her book *The New Community*, she lists the marks of the church. They are also the aims of a catechetical ministry that will lead to faithful stewardship. They include: a commitment to the poorest, the weakest, the most abused members of the human family; a commitment to the life of dialogue; a commitment to a critical contemplation of one's own life and the life of one's faith community; a commitment to a life of reflection; and a commitment to times of solitude and silence. To tell the story of how these commitments are lived out in community is to illustrate the best of ascetical catechesis. It can begin with children; it must continue throughout our lifelong pilgrimage.

Chapter Seven

Life as Caring:
Pastoral Catechesis

One day while passing through our parish house I observed an amazing event. A small group of women had gathered in the parlor for tea and cucumber sandwiches. A highly intoxicated, dirty, unshaven young man wandered into their room, sat down on a comfortable sofa, and fell soundly asleep. They simply accepted his presence. Without any need to run over to do something in particular, they acknowledged that he needed sleep. One commented, "Perhaps he will be hungry when he awakes." Another filled a china plate with cucumber sandwiches and placed them next to him. When they had finished their afternoon of conversation and fellowship, they checked on his condition, and finding him still sleeping soundly, quietly left. One of them returned the next day to find the plate empty and next to it a poorly handwritten note that simply said, "Thank you"!

On another occasion I was leading a diocesan educational event at an inner-city church in Texas. At the close of the day, we had gathered for wine and cheese in the church parish hall. A local street woman wandered in carrying her bags. She filled a large plate with cheese and crackers, took two glasses of wine, and sat down between two of the workshop's participants. She told them her story and they listened. They filled her glass and she went over to the piano and for the next hour entertained the community. Quietly they took an offering for the woman and when she was ready to leave gave her a bag of food and the money in appreciation for her contribution to their community's life.

The liturgical dimension of practical theology reminds us that we are stewards of the Gospel, entrusted with the Good News of God. When we gather we experience the abundant life that results from the gift of God's grace and we are granted the faith to perceive it in our lives and history. As trustees of this unspeakable gift, we have an obligation to help others to become aware of this same experience in their lives, or, as we promise in our baptismal covenant, "to proclaim by word and example the Good News of God in Christ."

The moral dimension of practical theology reminds us that we are stewards of the material world in which we live. Each of us has received some gift of material wealth and possessions as well as the gift of the natural world and all its resources. As trustees of these gifts, we need to acknowledge that they have been given to us for the benefit of all and we have the obligation to use them on behalf of all humanity, or as we promise in our baptismal covenant, "to strive for justice and peace among all people, and respect the dignity of every human being."

The spiritual dimension of practical theology reminds us that we are stewards of time. As the trustees of time we are held accountable for how we date and live time from birth to death as well as the purposes for which we use this gift, or as we promise in our baptismal covenant, "to continue in the apostles' teaching and fellowship, in the breaking of bread and in the prayers; and to persevere in resisting evil and when we fall into sin, repent and return to the Lord."

The pastoral dimension of practical theology reminds us that we are stewards of our life situations and of our abilities. All too often we attribute our life situations to fate or luck and our abilities to heredity or our achievement. We live as if they are ours for our own advantageous use and enjoyment. But as trustees of our lives, we have an obligation to minister, to care for, and to serve all people, or as we promise in our baptismal covenant, "to seek and serve Christ in all persons, loving our neighbor as ourself." Stewardship of the gifts of the Spirit implies compassion and concern for the broken and the desperate, the disadvantaged.

The author of Mark did not think the suffering of Jesus was an unfortunate accident or a minor setback that soon would be overcome and all but obliterated by the resurrection. Those who expect of the Christian faith a deliverance from all future suffering and pain are warned by Mark's account of God's Good News that suffering is an integral part of the fate of the one we revere. Following Christ can hardly be understood as a guarantee that life will be nothing but painless and uninterrupted joy. For Mark, the path to glory for Jesus lay through the valley of the cross, and Jesus' followers are therefore armed not for the avoidance of suffering, but with the confidence that suffering, real and bitter though it be, is not the final word. Those who take the Gospel seriously are thus prepared to face the inevitable struggles and pain life brings and to survive them victoriously. To follow Christ means to be open to the pain and suffering, the confusions and despair of all those who come seeking help. To be stewards of the Gospel, explains the German theologian Dorothee Soelle, is to continually journey through four movements in time: to begin by becoming conscious and present to the cross in the lives of those who journey with us; to name the principalities and powers that lie behind their crosses; to image the resurrection God wills to bring to their crosses; and to open ourselves to will the taking up of our cross so that we might follow Christ our Lord.

Flannery O'Connor wrote to her friend Louise Abbot, "I think there is no suffering greater than what is caused by the doubts of those who want to believe. I know what torment this is, but I can only see it, in myself anyway, as the process by which faith is deepened. A faith that just accepts is a child's faith and all right for children but eventually you have to grow up religiously as every other way, though some never do."[17] On another occasion she wrote, "What people don't realize is how much religion costs. They think faith is a big electric blanket when of course it is a cross."[18]

Practical theology and catechesis speaks of experience, of participation in the lives of others. Douglas Anderson in his book *New Approaches to Family Pastoral Care* (published by Fortress Press) tells a parable about the three little pigs. To retell it, years had passed since the crisis with the wolf and they had settled down comfortably in their brick house in the suburbs. Gradually boredom set in. Each of them felt empty. One day they decided that what they were missing was love and they set out to discover love's meaning. The first little pig went to the university library and read all she could on the subject of love. When she had finished she had learned a great deal about love but still felt empty. The second little pig read in the church newsletter that a famous pig was coming to church to deliver a series of lectures on love. He attended all the lectures and was filled with enthusiasm. His emotional high, however, only lasted about four days and then life returned to what it had been before. The third little pig invited other pig families to her home. They shared their life stories, their joys and sorrows. They met regularly and soon discovered that they cared about each other deeply. One evening after everyone had left the third little pig said to the others, "Now I know what love is, for I have experienced it."

Christian faith is understood by experiencing the mystery of life in Christ. The Christian faith is a way of life. To be Christian one must be a doer of the Word, not a mere spectator or listener.

Among all the church's devotions, the one that most vividly encourages and fosters our active sharing in the life and ministry of Christ is the *Way of the Cross*. In this devotion we become pilgrims of the way by walking with Christ along the *via dolorosa*, the way to Calvary.

Not long ago I led a retreat for a congregation during the first weekend in Lent. It was to be based on the *Way of the Cross* as found in *The Book of Occasional Services*. On Friday night persons of all ages gathered at a retreat house some thirty minutes from where they lived. Following a simple supper, we divided into fourteen groups, each representing one station of the cross: (1) Jesus is condemned to death—injustice; (2) Jesus takes up his cross—agony; (3) Jesus falls the first time—danger; (4) Jesus meets his afflicted mother—grief; (5) The cross is laid on Simon of Cyrene—friendlessness; (6) A woman wipes the face of Jesus—compassion; (7) Jesus falls a second time—oppression; (8) Jesus meets the women of Jerusalem—sorrow; (9) Jesus falls a third time—affliction; (10) Jesus is stripped of his garments—poverty; (11) Jesus is nailed to the cross—crime; (12) Jesus dies on the cross—dying; (13) The body of Jesus is placed in the arms of his mother—suffering; (14) Jesus is laid in the tomb—abandonment.

Each group was directed to make a symbolic representation of their station; to create a dramatization of their station; and to reflect on the theme presented with each station and decide on some place in our community where that theme (for example: injustice, danger, or poverty) was manifested.

The next morning we got into cars and went to each of those places in the community and for five minutes were silently present. When we returned to the retreat center we went on the way of the cross. We sang between each station (the pictorial representations of each station had been placed around the retreat house ground; it took three hours to go the whole journey). As we stopped at each station a group dramatized its story and led a guided meditation that took us back to our morning visits. We were silent, we prayed, and we moved on.

That evening everyone was asked to discern at which station she or he felt closest to Christ. We divided into these new groups. Each group was asked to decide how they could bring Christ to that place in the community during Lent. At our closing Eucharist we made these commitments to ministry our offering. As stewards of God's grace, we would exemplify and manifest pastoral caring as our Lenten devotion. When we returned home we sought others who would like to express their stewardship during Lent by joining each ministry group. It was a holy Lent.

As George Herbert, the seventeenth century Anglican patron saint of pastoral care, once said, a pastor is one who carries a cross so that others might bear their own cross with hope.

Doops Momber is one of three characters in Will Campbell's new novel *The Glad River*. All three find themselves in the army against their will. One day Doops finds Kingston crying in the woods. He is simply present to this other man's torment and sorrow. However, before they return to the base Kingston asks, "Are you my friend?" "Friend," Doops replies, "That's a strange word. We'll have to see. But we're neighbors. Like I say we're neighbors. I know that much."[19] I could not help but reflect on Jesus' command, "Love your neighbor," love the one in need.

In the same novel Will Campbell has Doops's comments on community: "It's a bunch of folks getting along for some reason. Something holds them together. Something bad . . . . If we had met at the circus we probably wouldn't even have liked each other. But this damned army, this idiot war, holds us together. Being miserable and suffering holds folks together. But when things are easy and everything is going right, they drift apart."[20] Our common suffering holds us together. The gift of community comes to those who are willing to embrace the suffering of others. Then I read on. Doops reflects, "A Christian is someone who loves the Lord so much that he is willing to risk going to hell for the sake of the brethren."[21] Yes, the stewardship of our suffering is the will to suffer for another who suffers, I thought.

Children know what suffering is and children can minister to suffering. I recall one evening during Lent when I was conducting an informal family Eucharist. The Gospel was on suffering and I asked the community if they could name people they knew who suffered. The children appeared to have less difficulty than the adults. Then one little girl hugged her father and said, "My daddy is suffering, but he won't tell anybody." In embarrassment he said, "Beth you're going to hug me to death." "No, daddy," she exclaimed, "I'm hugging you to life." We moved on and they named ways they could bring Christ to those they knew who were suffering. Once again the children seemed more able than the adults to name a concrete act of ministry. Pastoral catechesis with children is not difficult. It means sharing ministry with them; it means including them in our ministry; it means making them aware of our ministry; and it means encouraging them to minister and supporting them in it. In these informal, but intentional ways, we aid children to see their lives as stewards of God's love and care.

Stanley Hauerwas, the Notre Dame ethicist, once commented that Christians must be concerned with developing forms of caring and support, the absence of which seems to make abortion a necessity in our society. In particular, he said, Christians should, in their own communities, make clear that the role of parent is one we all share, single and married alike. Thus the woman who is pregnant and carrying a child need not be the one to raise it. We must be a people who stand ready to receive and care for any child, not just as if it were one of ours, but because in fact each *is* one of ours. Christians are to be the kind of people who are ready and willing to receive and welcome children into the world, for children are a sign of the trustworthiness of God's creation and God's unwillingness to abandon the world to the powers of darkness. To be stewards of God's creative power is to welcome new life and preserve all life. To be stewards of God's love is to love and care for all God's children. The pastoral catechesis of children demands that they be incorporated into a community that wants and respects them, for children are a community's sign that life—in spite of its hardships and tragedy—is worthwhile and that life is a gift of God for which we are to be faithful stewards.

Hospitality and compassion are at the heart of pastoral care. We all may be wounded, said Henri Nouwen, but our wounds can become the source of healing when we put our broken, lonely, incomplete selves in the service of others. Jean Vanier in his moving book *Followers of Jesus* tells of Marjorie Conners from Patricia House in Canada, who died a few years ago. Marjorie used to receive into her small bedraggled room in downtown Montreal alcoholics and the "dregs" of society. There was great compassion in her, he explained. When she introduced you to a prostitute it was as if she were introducing you to a queen. You experienced her love and respect for the image of God within every human being.

Vanier lives out his ministry with the mentally retarded. He does not permit future teachers of those who will care for the retarded to see them as *cases*. For him they are simply persons in the image of God who, like all of us, have been wounded and, therefore, like all of us, need kindness, understanding, compassion, and respect, not rejection, pity, or condescension. He makes clear that in our caring we must be careful not to want to help people; when we want to help others we have a tendency to make them dependent on us and our help. To paraphrase his thoughts: We can too easily inflate our personalities by giving and in doing so we may hurt rather than help another. We must give of ourselves or better share, not with a feeling of superiority, but as instruments of Christ who do not possess in our own right, but as stewards who must render accounts to God. Whatever possessions we have do not really belong to us, but to Christ. For anything we give through our caring, the glory is not for us but for him, the thanksgiving should not come to us nor to the church but to him.[22]

Our pastoral life in the church aims to share an authentic love that draws humanity and God together. Such love is not a feeling; it is an act of the will. Jesus never said that we were to *like* our neighbors; but he did say that we were to act on behalf of our neighbor's good. And who is our neighbor? Anyone in need, even and perhaps especially those we do not like, those from whom we are estranged. Jesus does not exhort us to wait for an emotional feeling. As a matter of fact, mature believers do not let their emotions control them; they control their emotions. The pastoral love to which we are called is an active caring and concern for the intellectual, emotional, physical, and spiritual well-being of our neighbors.

Such pastoral love is unconditional, that is, it is given on the basis of need and not on the basis of deserving. It is unconditional also in the sense that it is given regardless of the response of the recipient, that is, it is given freely without any expectation of gain. And it is sacrificial, which may mean giving one's life for another, but it may also mean the willingness to sacrifice our ideas for the sake of harmony in the church, the willingness to sacrifice an hour each week to visit the elderly or prepare a meal for a shut-in; the willingness to sacrifice the architectural beauty of our parish house so we can have a soup kitchen and provide a place for the homeless to sleep; the willingness to sacrifice personal pleasures for the sake of the needy. And last, it is the result of a rational decision. True love is not sentimental concern, but the result of hard moral thinking. It is an act of the will.

When considering our pastoral ministry we cannot divide the world into sacred and profane. Our pastoral ministry of active caring, caring that enables persons to be aware of the gift of God's love, extends to the practice of law, education, and medicine; the management of business, industry, and government; the labor of farm, assembly line, and store; the creations of stage, screen, and art gallery. Each and every one of us can be the sacrament of God by expressing the grace we have received in our care for others. From my perspective one of our most important pastoral concerns must be education. If we really care for people, we will be concerned for their growth and development, we will make a major effort to aid them in their journey to maturity, we will seek their enlightenment, free them from prejudice and ignorance, we will endeavor to give them tools to interpret Scripture intellectually, to think theologically, and to make rational moral decisions. There is no more important pastoral ministry than that of the catechist. We need to equip an ever-larger group of adults, mature in faith and life, with the knowledge, skills, and spiritual maturity necessary to help children, youths, and other adults on their journey into Christ.

Locks Bowman, Episcopal priest, longtime friend, advocate and helper of catechists (he would say teachers), has prophetically revealed our benign neglect of this essential ministry as well as our neglect of those to whom the Spirit's gifts were given that they might manifest God's grace through teaching. If we are to truly care for children, we must be concerned about the lives of maturing adults. The test of our caring can be observed in our catechetical ministry. The test of caring for children can be observed in the time, talent, and money we give to caring for adults and enabling them to be catechists.

Gifts of the Spirit

We are responsible for each other. Caring for each other is to be our way of life. "Whatever gift each of you have received, use it in service to one another, like good stewards dispensing the grace of God in its varied forms" (1 Pet. 4:10). As Paul put it, to each is granted the manifestations of the Spirit for the common good. God's grace is given us not for our sole enjoyment, but in trust to be used for and passed on to others. We are the channels of God's grace to others. Each of us is to be an agent of God's unmerited liberating and reconciling love. We do that through acts of caring, of service, of ministry. The gifts and graces in our lives are never given us for our sole benefit or enjoyment; they are given us as a blessing for the community. Recognizing that any constructive, caring, serving contribution by any member of the community is recognized by Saint Paul as a spiritual gift, some gifts are directed toward the growth of wisdom and understanding, some toward the psychosocial well-being of the community, some toward the physical welfare of the community and its members, and some toward the spiritual health of the community. Spiritual gifts are given by God for the building up of the community.

Vincent Donovan, a Roman Catholic Holy Ghost Father, went as a missionary to East Africa and there he explains, in his moving book *Christianity Rediscovered*, he did just that. It is not easy to grow up in North America and understand Christian faith. There is so much in our culture that is antithetical to the faith witnessed to in the Scriptures. But Africans, like early Christians, share a conviction that the human experience is communal, that is, individuals are subordinate to life-in-community. African Christians share a deep sense of belonging to one another and the obligation to bear responsibility for one another. The idea is not new. Pascal once wrote, "One Christian is no Christian." Cyprian wrote, "Outside the Church there is no salvation," which simply meant there was no genuine human life apart from life in community. Human life is life for one another.

Father Donovan discovered that within these African Christian communities there was no competition. No one tried to stand out; in fact, no one wanted to stand apart. The community would recognize the most talented, the brightest, the most attractive, took pride in their membership in the community and rested their hope on these gifted people bringing honor to the community. People with lesser gifts were equally accepted and affirmed and simply expected to contribute according to their gifts. With no one seeking individual aggrandizement and everyone striving in the use of their gifts for excellence, not only is every person valued, wanted, and cared for, but communal well-being is insured. In discussing how these gifts were used in the gathered community for worship, he observed that some naturally assumed responsibility to pray the prayers, for they had the gift of bringing an awareness of God's blessings to the community. Some had the ability to explain and answer questions—they were the teachers; some were eloquent and could stir the people to belief and action—they became the preachers; some had the gift of leading singing, and so forth, but each had something unique to offer to all the others.

But Father Donovan also discovered that in each community one person was recognized as the sign of the unity that existed among them; this person had the gift of bringing the community to life and enabling its members to contribute their varied gifts. This person was their priest and presided at their rituals so that the community might function. This person was not necessarily the best teacher, reader, singer, prayer, or preacher nor did this person assume any of these roles. As priest, this person, chosen by the community, bore the symbols of the community, and signified for them the meaning of their life together by enabling the community to carry out its functions and actions.[23] They exemplified what James Fenhagen, dean of General Theological Seminary, once called mutual ministry.[24]

The church is called as the body of Christ to be God's sacrament in the world. As such, it is called to offer to the world a sign of God's kingdom. When the world looks at the church it should see a manifestation of the community for which we all seek and long. The church is to be a community of faith, hope, and love that brings to all people an experience of freedom, reconciliation, wholeness, discernment, compassion, hospitality, intimacy, and well-being. This community itself is a gift of the Spirit.

John Koenig's book *Charismata: God's Gifts for God's People* (published by Westminster) is the most helpful book I have ever read on the gifts of the Spirit. I am in his debt and I hope I have not distorted his scholarship or misrepresented his insights. Koenig points out that Paul's list of spiritual gifts is really limitless. Some, however, that Paul specifically mentions are wisdom (insight into the truth of the Gospel and its implications for life), knowledge (understanding the tradition and the significance of historical events), extraordinary faith (perceiving the presence and activity of God in our life and lives), miraculous works (making known the healing power of God's love), prophecy (knowing and being able to express the mind of God), discernment of spirits (right judgment as to the will of God), speaking in tongues and its interpretation (freedom from one's own consciousness and openness to the spiritual dimension of life), and oversight (enabling the community to carry out its functions and actions).

These gifts of the Spirit are given so that a variety of necessary functions in the community might be realized. Some may be apostles (those able to witness in word and deed to the Gospel), prophets (those able to communicate God's admonition, direction, and encouragement), teachers (those able to draw insight from what God has done and said), evangelists (those able to help others see the grace of God in their lives and in history), miracle workers (those able to help persons open themselves to the presence and activity of God), pastors (those able to perform acts of mercy, caring, and service), and administrators (those able to aid the community in living a life of ministry in the world). Paul provides guidelines to judge these spiritual gifts in the form of the fruits they will bear, namely: love, joy, peace, patience, kindness, goodness, faithfulness, gentleness, self-control. The list of spiritual gifts, of course, is endless—so are the functional roles in which they can be manifested—but the fruits will always be signs of God's kingdom come, God's sovereign will realized, God's community actualized.

Paul also speaks of the gifts such as healing. In this regard it is important to note that he stresses the gifts of healing received from God through the Spirit and not the gift of the healer. We are granted healing so that we might use our health for the benefit of others. Health is a gift, and we are accountable for its use. Our strength can support another weakness, our well-being can be used to care for others in need. Indeed, for Paul every life situation presents us with gifts for ministry. Just as marriage is a gift, so is singleness. While singleness may not always be our choice, it always presents us with a gift for ministry. Bearing children offers us a gift, a potential for ministry, but so does the inability to bear children. We need to recognize our human condition as gift and recognize the potential for ministry it offers us as a gift. That is how Paul understood his celibacy; that is also how Paul understood his "thorn in the flesh." Every apparent negative in our lives suggests a gift in the form of a possibility for service. Every limitation, handicap, burden, deprivation; our brokenness, incompleteness, suffering, tribulations become the context for a gift of the Spirit making it possible for us to be a source of healing, a source of comfort, courage, hope, and blessing for others who share our infirmities.

All gifts are inspired and distributed by the Spirit, by God, to equip Christ's body, the church, for mutual ministry or service. As Paul wrote to the community at Corinth, "To each is given the manifestation of the Spirit *for the common good*" (1 Cor. 12:7).

While we all have been given different gifts, one, the most important and one we all share, is the gift of love. Without love, our acknowledgment and use of separate gifts can be a worthless display of egotism or can be used to cause division among us. Ultimately it is not our varied gifts that count most, valuable as they are, but our love for each other. "Pursue love and desire spiritual gifts," Paul counseled the community at Corinth (1 Cor. 14:12). That is, we are to put our primary energy into loving the neighbor, through the use of our gifts.

Pastoral Catechesis

At the foundation of what Dean Fenhagen has called mutual ministry is enablement, or equipping persons for ministry. Enablement is helping others to recognize the gifts they have been given (women and men, children, youths, and adults), aiding them in the development of their gifts, and encouraging and supporting their use for the benefit of others. One of the great heresies of the contemporary church is the identification of the ordained person as the minister. The sign of a healthy congregation is the number of persons who are being educated and supported in caring for one another, being equipped for ministry. There is no more important ministry than being able to discern and affirm the gifts in those with whom we minister. What is more meaningful than making others aware of the love, truth, and beauty they reveal to us? We live in a day when many doubt their self-worth. Few realize that they are lovable, and able to love. We can save lives by seeing the image of God in others and helping them to see the spiritual gifts they have to share. Ministry is calling forth the hidden gifts in all people and celebrating with them the gifts they bring and give to us.

Within every congregation are those who have the gift to tell stories, to create, to speak, to solve problems, to resolve conflict, to organize, to plan, to raise money, to dance and sing, to see reality clearly and make it visible to others, to care for the sick, hurt, and suffering, to attract the lapsed and unchurched, to reconcile the estranged, to liberate the oppressed, to bring justice to the needy, to be a friend to strangers, to bring compassion to the broken and companionship to the lonely. None of us, no matter how tragic our own lives, is without some spiritual gift necessary for ministry. Indeed, the divorced, the grieving, the alcoholic, each can best serve those who suffer as they suffer. If we see behind our lives the gracious hand of God and acknowledge our human situation and our talents as spiritual gifts, then we can be God's faithful stewards.

One role of pastoral catechesis is to help people to identify and acknowledge their gifts and graces. Another is to aid them to develop those gifts and graces to the fullest. Pastoral catechesis can also serve to aid persons in their search for new gifts and graces to the end that the church's ministry might grow and expand. Pastoral catechesis with children implies helping them to discern the gifts of the Spirit in their lives and equipping them to use these gifts faithfully as stewards of God's grace in the service of others.

I recall an evening in a local parish when children, youths, and adults gathered to consider their lives as stewards of God's gifts for pastoral ministry. When people arrived they gathered around tables of eight persons with the aim of having as many generations represented as possible. During the meal they each, beginning with the oldest, shared their faith biography. Following the meal they were sent to the nave to pray, to ask God to reveal to them some concrete ministry to which their congregation was being called. As each received some insight they returned to the parish hall and wrote that ministry on newsprint.

While the community gathered they sang hymns to celebrate their growing vision of ministry. Then a lay person shared Paul's letter on the variety of spiritual gifts. Each was to think of a gift or grace in their life to which they were being called to be stewards. They wrote their name, address, telephone number, and the gift on a three-by-five-inch card. They also were to think of some part of the human body that was representative of their gift. Those familiar with anatomy helped the others consider what the heart, glands, intestine, and so forth contributed to the life of the body. They made a representation of that part of the anatomy and put it on a huge human body drawn on the wall. A physician commented humorously when they were finished that the body had a chance to live but probably would never reproduce. They looked at the body with all its gifts and graces and then nominated and elected a group of ten people whose responsibility it would be to see that all had the opportunity to develop and use their gifts in the ministry outlined on the newsprint. Then they celebrated Eucharist together, commissioned those who were to enable the community for ministry, and offered both their vision and their various gifts and graces to God as their sacrifice of thanksgiving. *That* is pastoral catechesis.

Chapter Eight

Postscript

I'm finished, but haunted by a sense of not being finished. Like any Christian, I have tried to be transparent and vulnerable in the hope that you will risk honesty and openness in your search for truth. Like any priest, I have tried to faithfully proclaim the Gospel in the hope that your faith might be enhanced and enlivened. Like any professor, I have tried to rationally profess what I believe at this moment in the hope that you will be stimulated to think for yourself. But have I? Have I been faithful to Christ and his church? Have I offered anything of enduring value to you who share with me the mystery of faith and come searching for insight? I pray that I have. I also pray that where I have failed, God will redeem. May you have heard God's Word through my faltering speech and yet may none of my words have gone unjudged by God's redeeming Spirit.

Still, I'm not satisfied. My work seems so inadequate. Perhaps I need to offer a warning, for there is a power that comes to those who write books they do not deserve. It comes in the form of a Sufi story about the folk hero Nasrudin (the Sufis are Muslim mystics). It seems that Nasrudin was seated in his home one day. A neighbor came to visit and asked, "May I please borrow your donkey?" Now Nasrudin did not want to loan out his donkey so he replied, "I'm very sorry but I just loaned out my donkey yesterday." At that

139

point the donkey brays in the barn. The neighbor thinks, now I've got him, "Nasrudin, what is that that I hear in the barn?" "Sir," replies Nasrudin, "are you going to believe me or a donkey?"[25]

In the spirit of that ancient tale, let me share four necessary warnings to anyone who might have been attracted to the thesis of this book. First, I have written this book from what I intend to be an Anglican perspective, aware that it is only one peculiar way of looking, making sense, and acting. Like each and every communion within the Christian tradition, Anglicans have their unique starting point (which, interestingly, is typically both our Achilles' heel and best contribution to the one, holy, catholic, and apostolic church for whose unity we all pray).

If you will permit me an unfair caricature: there are the free churches, who begin with individual interpretations of the Holy Scripture, for example the Baptists; there are the confessional churches, who begin with a confessional document, such as the Lutheran Augsburg Confession or the Presbyterian Westminster Confession; there are the pragmatic churches, who begin with personal experience, such as the United Methodists; there are the doctrinal churches, who begin with the theological teachings of the magisterium, such as the Roman Catholic Church; and there are the liturgical churches, who begin with a prayer book, such as the Anglican or Episcopal Church.

It is, therefore, *The Book of Common Prayer* (1979) that provides me with a starting point for engaging in practical theology. *Lex orandi, lex credendi,* "the law of praying is the law of believing." My theology arises out of the patterns of worship established in the prayer book. How Anglicans symbolically act in their rituals is what they believe or at least are supposed to believe (some Episcopalians are not aware of that). Thus it was natural for me to begin with a discussion of baptism to establish a theological foundation and understanding of stewardship; it was natural to turn to baptismal initiation for clues to the process of catechesis; it was natural to make the first dimension of practical theology liturgical catechesis; and it was natural to continually make reference to the liturgy throughout the other chapters of the book. As a committed Anglican, I could not do it any other way. Others will make different contributions to this important subject and they will do it from their own perspectives. We need each other.

But there is another Anglican emphasis that has particular significance for this book on stewardship: God created everything and it is good. There can be no split between the material and the spiritual, the sacred and the secular. All of life must be understood from an incarnational perspective. God embraces the totality of life in all its ambiguity and paradox. The extraordinary love of God is to be found in the ordinary, the particularity of the concrete. Life is sacramental. The spiritual is always expressed in the material and the material provides necessary expression for the spiritual. The church is the sacrament of Christ: it must embody and manifest in the world the presence and activity of God.

That is somewhat difficult for some to understand. One cradle Episcopalian wrote a letter to the editor of *The Communicant*, the newspaper of the Diocese of North Carolina, "I am not a member of the Episcopal Church because I want moral, social or political guidance. I am a member of the Episcopal Church because I need its spiritual guidance." Surely that writer could not have reflected seriously on *The Book of Common Prayer*; indeed, it is difficult to know where he has been all these years. I suspect that his understandings of stewardship are also in conflict with those of the Episcopal Church. In any case, I have tried to be faithful to the Anglican tradition in dealing with the issues of practical theology, stewardship, and catechetical ministry. For the sake of my Anglican friends, I trust I have done so. For the rest of my friends, I warn you about the Anglican biases and presuppositions in this book.

Second, I have chosen to use the language of catechetics. There are other ways to talk, for example the language of religious education, Christian education, Christian nurture, Christian religious education, church or parish education, or religious instruction. Each has its advocates. Each makes an important contribution to the church's ministry. Each should be taken seriously. Catechetics has a long history; the others a much shorter history. While Protestants generally sought a new language, Roman Catholics kept to the language of catechetics. Recently liberal Roman Catholics have sought to adopt historic Protestant language. Many of these folk are my respected friends. They object to my wanting to use the language of catechetics because in their experience it has been associated with the ecclesiastical establishment's conservative efforts at doctrinal indoctrination; it has been associated with what some call theological imperialism or the attempt to place education under the control of theology; and it has been associated with oppressive efforts to maintain societies with unjust sociopolitical and economic policies. It would be foolish not to admit that this has been so. Indeed, that fact presents us with a warning and a challenge to guard against such distortions. Still I do not believe these distortions make an adequate case for the abandonment of such language.

Therefore, I have committed myself to reform and reintroduce the language of catechetics. I do so, perhaps, because of its liturgical foundations, but also because it provides a sense of continuity with the past in a day when our efforts are shallow because we are singularly enamored of the understandings and ways of our scientific, post-Enlightenment, modern age. It also offers us a way of thinking and acting as a tradition-bearing community of faith, in a day when our efforts are inadequate because we are solely enamored of a modern, secular, social-science understanding of development and instruction. Further, it provides us with a way of talking and acting that goes back to a time when the church was one, to be used today when the church is pained by its divisions and seeking unity. Others are offering important critiques of this catechetical school of which I am representative and some are offering useful alternatives. I think of Thomas Groome, Gabriel Moran, Mary Boys, Maria Harris, Gloria Durka, and many others. I do not dismiss their work, in fact, I am continually learning from them. No one perspective is completely adequate. Mine is only one among many, but it is the one to which I have committed my mind, heart, and labor.

A third warning is the Anglican understanding about the relationship of Christ and culture, which is assumed throughout this book, though it is perhaps hidden. H. Richard Niebuhr, in his classic *Christ and Culture* (published by Harper & Row), discussed five possible relationships between Christ and culture. These are "Christ against Culture," which rejects culture, regards the world as evil, and requires the church to separate itself from the culture so as to offer an alternative for life; "Christ of Culture," which sees no tension between them, blesses the culture, and accommodates itself to the culture; "Christ above Culture," which envisions a possible synthesis and defends a both/and, rather than an either/or, position; "Christ and Culture," which establishes a dualistic, paradoxical relationship, an in-but-not-of position; and last, "Christ Transforming Culture," which understands its responsibility as being in the world in order to transform it; that is, to be a sacrament in the world. As Niebuhr points out in his discussion of the last position, it finds its fullest expression in the work of the nineteenth-century Anglican theologian, F. D. Maurice. I join myself to this Anglican theological tradition.

The fourth warning is found in the basic assumption that underlies the catechetical model as I have described it, namely, the presence of a story-formed community of faith. Others who share this perspective, such as C. Ellis Nelson and Craig Dykstra, both Presbyterians, can be criticized for the same assumption. My complete theory is based upon the existence of such a community. I have described its characteristics: it shares a common memory or story; it shares a common vision and holds to common terminal and instrumental values; it shares a common authority as well as ethical and theological norms; it shares common rituals; and, most important, it shares a common life together that is more like a family than a voluntary association or institution.

There have been some who have said that they do not know a local congregation in which everyone shares or is committed to a common story, vision, authority, and rituals. People, they say, do not belong to churches for such reasons: churches are pluralistic and therefore relativistic. For most folk individual freedom of belief and action is more important than communal authority and responsibility. But perhaps even more significant is the contention that churches are only voluntary associations that people join and leave at will. If the church does not meet their needs, they seek another that does or simply drop out. Churches are goal-oriented, task-oriented, highly structured bylaw-ridden institutions to whom persons give limited and contractual loyalty, in which they play limited roles, and in which their worth is judged by participation and contribution.

As one thoughtful critic of my model asked: "Does it even make sense to use the communal and historic imagery of a faith community in a society ruled by assumptions and conceptualizations of modern institutions?" My answer is that it has to make sense even if it does not now exist, for without a community of faith all our efforts are in vain.

Herbert O'Driscoll, now warden of the College of Preachers in Washington, D.C., a few years ago addressed the United States Episcopal bishops. To paraphrase him: We live in a time in history in which we are like a child in a womb desperately longing to see an outline of the face of her whom we will meet in the future. And then, he continued, this feminine image is extremely helpful (interestingly, another characteristic of the Anglican perspective), for if the church is to be faithful to its Lord and survive, it will have to cease being a masculine, task-oriented, goal-oriented institution and become more of a feminine, nurturing, caring community. We will have to become a community in which we find our roots in a story and our value in our *being*, in which we give to each other whatever love demands even as we commit our total personality. We should be a community where intuitive subjective experience complements an objective intellectual ordering of life. We are called in the church, he said, to exchange a neat system for a spiritual journey. In the midst of this time, he said, we feel a pain in the gut of our culture and our church, but what we need is the faith to see that it is a pregnancy and not a malignancy.

He's right, of course. At least I've cast my lot with him and others who believe that the place to begin is to strive to meet the necessary characteristics of a faith community so that the gift of community might be ours. I make no apology, therefore, for the assumption of a community of faith, but I do warn you that without it most of what we have discussed in this book will be frustrated from the start.

Permit me then to close with two passages from letters of Flannery O'Connor. "I think the church," she wrote, "is the only thing that is going to make the terrible world we are coming to endurable; the only thing that makes the church endurable is that it is somehow the body of Christ and that on this we are fed. It seems to be a fact that you have to suffer as much from the church as for it but if you believe in the divinity of Christ you have to cherish the world at the same time that you struggle to endure it."[26]

And last, "I was once, five or six years ago, taken by some friends to have dinner with Mary McCarthy and her husband, Mr. Broadwater. (She just wrote that book, *A Charmed Life*.) She departed the Church at the age of 15 and is a Big Intellectual. We went at eight and at one, I hadn't opened my mouth once, there being nothing for me in such company to say. The people who took me were Robert Lowell and his now wife, Elizabeth Hardwick. Having me there was like having a dog present who had been trained to say a few words but overcome with inadequacy had forgotten them. Well, toward morning the conversation turned on the Eucharist, which I, being the Catholic, was obviously supposed to defend. Mrs. Broadwater said when she was a child and received the Host, she thought of it as the Holy Ghost, He being the 'most portable' person of the Trinity; now she thought of it as a symbol and implied that it was a pretty good one. I then said, in a very shaky voice, 'Well, if it's a symbol, to hell with it.' That was all the defense I was capable of but I realize now that this is all I will ever be able to say about it, outside of a story, except that it is the center of existence for me; all the rest of life is expendable."[27]

I share Flannery's experience and convictions. It is because of them, I suppose, that I have had the audacity—or perhaps it's the courage—to write this book. I have written it, as I have written all my books, for me. I hope it is also for you. Writing it has brought me to a new place in my pilgrimage. Now I will have to face new questions, conflicts, and problems. May it do the same for you as we journey together into Christ, a people of God gratefully and faithfully living upon the gifts of God.

Notes

1. Sally Fitzgerald, ed., *The Habit of Being* (New York: Random House, 1980), pp. 477–78.
2. Julian of Norwich, *Showings*, trans. Edmund Colledge and James Walsh (New York: Paulist Press, 1978), p. 335.
3. Adapted from *The Book of Common Prayer* (1979).
4. Ibid., pp. 304–5.
5. Regis Duffy, *Real Presence* (San Francisco: Harper & Row, 1982), p.10.
6. See: Tad Guzie, *The Book of Sacramental Basics*, (New York: Paulist Press, 1981).
7. Quoted in Duffy, *Real Presence*, p. 16.
8. See: Urban Holmes, *Turning to Christ* (New York: Seabury Press, 1982).
9. See: Thomas Groome, *Christian Religious Education* (San Francisco: Harper & Row, 1982), p. 19.
10. See: William Dalgliesh, *Models for Catechetical Ministry* (Washington, D.C.: United States Catholic Conference, 1982).
11. "The Faith of Children," an interview with Robert Coles, *Sojourners*, 12 May 1982, pp. 12–16.
12. Godfrey Diekmann, "Barakah Award Address," *Worship* 51 (July 1977):371.
13. Urban T. Holmes, "Responsive to the Word of God," *Sewanee Alumni News*, January 1980, p. 13.
14. Erich Fromm, *To Have or to Be?* (New York: Harper & Row, 1976).
15. Richard Foster, *The Celebration of Discipline* (San Francisco: Harper & Row, 1978), pp. 78–83.

16. See Thomas Merton, *Contemplation in a World of Action* (Garden City, N.Y.: Doubleday Image Books, 1973).
17. Fitzgerald, *Habit of Being*, p. 477.
18. Ibid., p. 354.
19. Will D. Campbell, *The Glad River* (New York: Holt, Rinehart & Winston, 1982), p. 12.
20. Ibid., p. 59.
21. Ibid., p. 308.
22. See Jean Vanier, *Followers of Jesus* (New York: Paulist Press, 1976).
23. Vincent J. Donovan, *Christianity Rediscovered* (Notre Dame, Ind.: Fides/Claretian, 1978), pp. 144–53.
24. See James Fenhagen, *Mutual Ministry* (New York: Seabury Press, 1977).
25. Idries Shah, *The Exploits of the Incomparable Mulla Nasrudin* (New York: Dutton, 1972), p. 22.
26. Fitzgerald, *Habit of Being*, p. 90.
27. Ibid., pp. 124–125.

also by JOHN H. WESTERHOFF III

Will Our Children Have Faith?

"To read a book that sparkles with ideas, provokes arguments, and conveys with clarity deep convictions is a joy."—*Theology Today*
144 pages   paperback

Liturgy and Learning Through the Life Cycle

"I wish I could require every pastor to read this book. It is the most interesting handbook on worship that I have seen in many years."—John S. Setterlund, *Augsburg Book Newsletter*
192 pages   hardcover

Inner Growth/Outer Change

An Educational Guide to Church Renewal

"Excellent material on the place of catechesis and liturgy in this process of 'embodying the word.'"—*New Review of Books and Religion*
176 pages   paperback

Learning Through Liturgy

"This book will stimulate your thinking, add to your knowledge, and perhaps disturb some of your presuppositions for education in the church. It deserves careful, thoughtful attention."—*Church and Synagogue Libraries*
208 pages   paperback

The Spiritual Life

Learning East and West

"A stimulating dialogue [with John D. Eusden]. Mr. Eusden offers rich insights he has gained from his contact with Zen Buddhism, while Mr. Westerhoff explores his knowledge of the Western religious tradition."—*Catholic Periodical and Literature Index*
134 pages   hardcover

Christian Believing

Volume 1 of the Church's Teaching Series

"A book to be shared by Christians of many beliefs and traditions."—*the Church Militant*
144 pages   hardcover and paperback

Seabury Service Center · Somers, CT 06071